CAMPING
LIKE CRAZY

Books by T. Morris Longstreth

CAMPING
LIKE CRAZY

By

T. MORRIS LONGSTRETH

Illustrations by

HEMAN FAY, JR.

THE MACMILLAN COMPANY
New York · 1953

To my friend

HARRIE B. PRICE III

of Flying Moose Lodge
that other
"Camp with a Difference"

CAMPING
LIKE CRAZY

CHAPTER I

That was the most terrific day I ever lived. Up till then, I mean.

All morning we thought Camp Chesunquoik was sunk. Mr. Wieldy, head of the Camp, had the mumps. My elephant, Dot, was missing. Lem Higgity, who was running things, had taken Downy and Stringy to notify the police. Only six fellows had signed up for the summer, and one of them, Murdo, had run off. Mrs. Lirrup, who wanted to bust up our camp because we disturbed the animals, had brought Sheriff Wickendorf to arrest me for not having an elephant license. And on top of all that, a Mr. Pickerel and forty boys, who were on their way home from a camp that had folded, stopped in to see my elephant. They had been attracted by her picture in the paper, which Bill Lister had drawn.

That was the big moment! If we could hook those boys, we'd be set up. But naturally they wouldn't stay

1

unless we could produce Dot. I'll never forget how Blister kept his nerve and turned the tables. Lem said it ought to be written down, so I did, on account of Lem being too busy. And Downy, who is our book-reader, said to call it *Elephant Toast* in honor of Silas Broadbeam's best dessert. That book ended when I ran out of paper, with me sitting at the head table, which was crosswise to the other tables like at a Scouts banquet, because I and Blister and Murdo had just been made junior counselors. And Lem was standing up to welcome the new fellows from the deceased camp.

I sure wished Pop could see me sitting there, with everybody staring at me because I owned Dot and Haru, my servant. There isn't one fellow in a hundred with a four-ton elephant and a Hindu working for him. It made me feel kind of high, though I had to be careful not to show it, or Blister, who was sitting next to me, would jump on me for being conceited. I never saw a boy so down on conceit in others as Blis, unless it's Murdo, who sat on the other side of me.

I wished Pop could see me because the joke was on him. When I left for camp, six days before this, Pop said he'd be satisfied if I brought home a camp letter. He didn't really think I'd get one in three years. And here I was a junior counselor in six days, and I wanted to see Pop's face when he heard.

I wished Mother could see me too, but on television or something like that. The last thing I wanted was for Mother to come and find out about Dot until I could break it to her gently. Mother had given me a postal to mail the day I reached camp to let her know I'd arrived safely, but I hadn't had time. So now I had to think up a nice way of telling her we had an elephant in the family, and Haru, and I couldn't seem to find the words.

After a while I got tired of thinking and switched back to Lem. He was doing all right. Lem claims he's no speaker, but he was explaining Camp Chesunquoik, the Camp with a Difference, to the new boys and making them feel at home. The fellows were paying pretty good attention considering the heat and their being full of elephant toast, and Dot trumpeting now and then for her lunch. It isn't every man who can talk down a hungry elephant, but Lem had most of their attention, except for an older boy who sat in front of me and a couple of twins beside him.

The older boy was acting in a funny way. Every time Dot trumpeted, this serious-looking boy rose a little from the bench, as if he had to see what was the matter, and the twins would laugh. The boy kept looking over to Haru, who was standing outside the tent listening to Lem. It looked like this boy was trying to catch Haru's eye, and I didn't get it.

Blis saw I was puzzled and whispered, "That's Gil Combs, from Florida. He's the one who saw Dot's picture in the paper and suggested to Mr. Pickerel that he bring the remains of their camp here. Next to me, and Dot of course, Mr. Wieldy owes him a debt of gratitude."

3

"That's all right," I said. "But what's he want with Haru?"

"Hasn't Gil talked to you yet?" Blis asked.

"How could he, with everything messing around! What's he want to talk about?"

"He wants Dot. His father, it seems, is animal-happy. The family isn't exactly wealthy, but people give Mr. Combs animals,—jaguars and kangaroos and armadillos. But he hasn't an elephant. So Gil expects to make him a present of Dot on his birthday. I think he said it's August first."

If Blis had hit me with a hammer, I couldn't have felt more stunned. The nerve of it! It was too silly to get mad about, but I was beginning to get mad, just the same.

"I thought I'd better wise you up," Blis whispered. "I saw the guy talking with Haru and they looked pretty thick."

"*Already?*"

"Sshh!" Blis stopped me, for I'd forgotten Lem was speaking. I looked at Gil Combs, the way a detective does in a murder mystery, to size him up, and what I saw didn't make me any happier. He was big for his age, whatever that was, about sixteen, I suppose, and very settled in his appearance. Confident, I guess you'd call it. He looked as if he had got everything he had ever wanted, and always would. Yet I don't mean smug. Just determined, in a nice way.

As I was studying him, Dot trumpeted again. She was

4

more emphatic than ever, and this time Gil Combs rose more than half way and motioned to Haru. Everybody noticed, and even Haru looked at Gil. Gil motioned again, and Haru nodded, and left in the direction of Dot's stockade.

Did that burn me up! I knew Haru was sore at me, because Murdo had caught him fleeing with Dot. That is how some people's minds work. But taking orders from a new boy was carrying it pretty far. Even Blis felt a little indignant and whispered, "All gall has been put together again. Caesar."

I could hardly wait for Lem to stop talking, so that I could explain to Gil Combs whose servant Haru was,— let alone whose elephant. What with Haru obeying him and Dot stopping trumpeting, Gil was so pleased that I couldn't stand looking at him, so I looked up at the top of the tent instead. A lot of flies and wasps were caught up there in the peak. I felt sorry for them, butting their single-track minds against the top when they could have tried something else after the first two or three hundred times. But all they knew how to do was buzz and butt,— buzz and butt.

Somehow they reminded me of Sheriff Wickendorf and *his* single-track mind. The only thing he could think of was to try and arrest me for having my elephant. It all came back, how he had grabbed for me and stepped into Mrs. Lirrup's geyser instead, and the funny look on his face as it half drowned him in Flit. I forgot where I was and bleated right out, and only realized what I was doing when Blis dug into me with his elbow and said in my ear, "Are you crazy?"

At the same time Murdo shoved his elbow into my other ribs and said, "What's so funny about that?"

I flushed up, and the twins snickered, and Lem pointed that state of Maine eye of his at me and said a little louder, "I repeat: Mr. Wieldy and I deeply deplore the sad accident which marked the tragic end of your previous camp . . ." Then I saw what I'd done. I'd laughed right out in their faces at the most solemn moment.

I couldn't help seeing Gil Combs staring at me in disgust. So I leaned my head way back again to look at the wasps and pretend they were what I'd been laughing at. I guess I made it plain for I heard no more snickers. A hornet had now joined the wasps. He was a determined fellow, like this Gil. I pretended he was Gil and said to myself: he's trying to find ways to get my Dot, and what happens is a sign. If he hasn't sense enough to back down and out, he won't succeed in getting Dot.

Well, that was exciting. Gil, the hornet, butted into the tent and was he mad! He'd haul away and I was scared that he'd remember there was all outdoors to fly in and he'd buzz off to Florida with Dot. But he didn't. The bigger the start he gave himself, the harder he'd butt the tent. He was twice as mad as the wasps, and he ripped around, and back-watered, and socked the old canvas again, till he must have had one swell headache. But it

6

didn't do him any good, and it was a sure sign Gil wouldn't get my elephant.

It was so exciting to see how it came out that I forgot everything else. I even clean lost track of what Lem was saying again, until Blister hissed in my ear, "Wake up, wake up, boobypate."

At the same time Murdo's elbow landed where I was black and blue. "Stand up, you old goat. Stand *up*, for Pete's sake," he said hoarsely. "Lem's introducing you."

Well, I took their word for it and stood up, though everything was in a kind of haze from looking up so long, and Lem said something I didn't hear and the twins snickered, and all the boys clapped. But they were laughing, too. I stood pretty still, considering I was dizzy, and suddenly Blis yanked at my shirt to pull me down on the bench, though I didn't understand why and went on standing.

"That's all, that's *enough*, mouse brain," Blis said.

Murdo pulled my wrist and said, "For crying out loud, sit *down*, will you. It's all over."

They all saw him and everybody roared, and Gil Combs was having a hard time of it not to smile, though he was still disgusted, and the twins were having convulsions. Then I heard Lem's voice above all the noise. "What is it, Silas?" he asked.

Silas Broadbeam said something.

"Excuse me, I can't hear!" Lem said.

"I said Mr. Keets's folks is here to see him, Mr. Lem."

Did that make my blood run cold! I knew what that

meant. Mother might be disturbed because she hadn't got the postal, but I couldn't see Pop bringing her all the way from Portland to the middle of Maine just to tell me. I guessed he'd read in the *Portland Crier* about my elephant. I knew Pop wouldn't drop business and come up for anything *less* than an elephant.

The laughing had suddenly stopped and I heard Lem say, "We'll excuse you, Keetsie. Please tell your parents that I shall join them in a few minutes."

If I could have grabbed one of Quizzy's spaceships and lit out for Neptune, I'd have done it. I looked over towards Silas and made out Pop and Mother standing in the sunlight, and knew I had to face the music.

As I raised my foot to lift it over the bench, my knee must have knocked Blis's iced tea glass. It spilled over him, and he made a remark, and the twins howled.

But you get past caring what happens.

CHAPTER II

I was afraid my knees would buckle, but I made it without stumbling over anyone except the twins. Something curious happened: Pop and Mother were glad to see me. I mean they didn't mention elephants or postals, and was that a relief!

Pop is tall, like me, only filled out more, and his forehead runs further up. It wrinkles some when he's sore, but now it was smooth as a pan. Mother kissed me warmly, as if I had just got back safe from Neptune, but I had kept shoving them out of sight of the tent, so it didn't matter.

"Father had a business call to Augusta a few minutes after you left, dear," Mother said. "So we haven't had word from you, or seen a paper. How are you?"

"Fine," I said. "I'm feeling swell."

"You look flushed," she said anxiously.

"I couldn't feel better."

"But I never saw your face so red. I hope it isn't fever."

"Nonsense!" Pop said. "He's been out in the sun." He looked at the row of tents and the great trees and the lake shining under the sun. "Some layout!" he said. "I thought Wieldy knew his business."

Mother had caught sight of the duffle which the new boys had left strewn about. "I'm afraid they're not teaching you to be orderly, dear. It's rather disgraceful."

"Forty new boys came in just a couple of hours ago, Mother," and I almost let out that they'd come because of my Dot but caught myself in time.

"Forty!" Pop whistled, the way he does when he's impressed. "That Wieldy's a hustler. I knew it. It's in his face. You'll have to work, sonny, to get your letter in this camp."

I opened my mouth to say I was a junior counselor and knock Pop over, for once. But I didn't, for he'd have to know why, and the one important thing was to see them off without hearing about Dot.

"Who was that able-looking young fellow addressing the campers?" Pop asked.

"Lem Higgity. He runs things for Mr. Wieldy . . . I mean he's next in charge."

"He looks as though he could get things done," Pop said.

"He does. He's a regular state-of-Mainer and the fellows like him."

"That fine-looking boy sitting on your right, who is he?" Mother asked.

"Blister . . . I mean Bill Lister. He draws. The newspapers print his drawings even. He's really good."

"And the dark boy on your left?" Mother asked.

"That's Murdo. He and I tent together. He's a swell guy." But I dropped Murdo there. I didn't think Mother would consider him so hot.

"Your cook's good-natured," Pop said. "That's rare. What's his name,—Broadbill?"

"Broadbeam, Silas Broadbeam. He has a lot of ancestors. I mean in different countries. He's descended from the something or other of Egypt, as well as Abyssinia, and Persia."

"But can he cook?" Mother asked.

"Cook!" I exclaimed. "Mr. Wieldy told us he was the best cook north of Cape Horn, but that's an understatement. You should taste his elephant toast!" I could have bit my tongue, for now they'd want to stay to supper.

"What on earth's that?" Mother asked.

"Just a dessert," I said.

"So that explains it!" Pop said. "I thought he was being funny. All fat people are funny."

"That's what I keep telling you," Mother said to Pop.

Pop let that one go and said, "Silas said something about your elephant."

I tried to laugh so it would sound natural. "Silas is fond of jokes, though sometimes they're hard to understand. Are you going back to Portland now?"

"Father has another call to make, but we ought to be

off," Mother said. "First though, I'd like to see your tent."

"It's not quite in order," I said. "We've been pretty busy this morning." I wondered what they'd say if they knew I'd almost been arrested.

"Just the same I'd like to see it," Mother said firmly. "After all, you've been here nearly a week . . . Mercy! What's that unearthly noise?"

It was Dot trumpeting. I glanced fast at Pop. His brow had wrinkled up like a washboard, and I knew I was in for it. "So Silas was joking, was he?" Pop asked drily.

Mother was glancing from Pop to me. "Don't tell me you *have* an elephant, dear! I don't mind the rabbits and the goat . . ."

"Out with it!" Pop ordered. "I knew something like this would happen."

You can't stall Pop when he means business, so I told about the little kid at the circus auction, and how I had bid five cents just to cheer him up, and all that. I made a big point of Dot's costing only a nickel, and that Camp Chesunquoik was feeding her.

"But that is hardly the point," Mother began anxiously.

"On the contrary, it is very much the point," Pop said. "Do you know how much it costs to feed an elephant a day?"

"I hope they don't allow you to go near the creature," Mother put in. "Who looks after it?"

"I have a servant from India."

13

"So *you* have a servant!" Pop said in a voice that'd curl your hair. "This grows more and more interesting."

"John, we must see about this," Mother interrupted. "I'm not going to have a son of mine trampled to death by elephants."

"Dot is as gentle as a kitten, Mother," I said. "Come, I'll introduce you to Haru, and he'll tell you the same thing."

So I walked them up the trail to the stockade. I could see that the reasonable price I'd paid for Dot and the camp's footing the food bill, had let considerable air out of Pop's tire. Mother was the jumpy one. But she's nervous about anything that has more than two feet.

Haru wasn't in the stockade, which suited me, for I was afraid he might be grumpy. Dot walked very stately to the rope across the opening and gave a big sniff, for she thought I was bringing her midday root beer. The sniff sounded like a transcontinental engine pulling out, and Mother backed off a couple of yards, but Pop stood his ground, I was glad to see.

"Watch how nicely she obeys me," I said, and ran under the rope and patted Dot's trunk and told her to lift me up. She did, and there I sat on her neck, with Pop and Mother cricking their necks staring up at me too astonished to tell me not to.

"Well, this beats me!" Pop said at last.

"It was Dot who attracted the new boys, Pop," I said. "She saved the camp from folding. And they've made me a junior counselor."

14

That shot went home. Pop's brow smoothed out and maybe I could have got him up on Dot, too, if Haru hadn't come up the trail with the pail of root beer. I saw right off that he was more sore at me than I feared even. He didn't bow, or call me Worthy Master. He stopped short, set down the pail of beer, and stood with his arms

folded in and out like a couple of snakes. Dot lifted her trunk and asked for the root beer and that scared Mother all over again.

"Isn't this animal dangerous?" Mother asked him.

"Yes, ma'am," Haru said very cooey and civil, and I wished I could choke him.

"Don't believe him, Mother!" I called down. "He's

15

sore on account of being caught while stealing my elephant."

"I have warned the young gentlemen," Haru continued. "The Terror of Crocodiles will someday lose her temper and tear him into shreds."

"That's not her name!" I told them. "She is Gem of the Ganges, Queen of All Created Elephants, and she carried children around for the circus."

"Why did the circus part with so valuable an animal?" Haru asked venomously. "I have warned the young gentleman for the last time."

Dot was growing more impatient for the root beer and leaned against the rope while she trumpeted.

"That settles it!" Mother exclaimed. "Surely this man knows more than you, dear. Please get down."

Unfortunately Dot's one idea was root beer, and she pressed a little harder against the rope. The trees it was tied to shook, and Pop looked uneasy.

"Whoa, Dot!" I commanded. "Back up. Give her the beer, Haru."

Dot paid no attention to me, for her trunk was straight out sniffing the delicious fumes of the beer just a trunk length away. Nor did Haru budge. Dot pressed harder and the rope creaked. It was a new rope and the trees would go first, and this would make a bad impression on Pop and Mother.

"Quit it, Dot!" I shouted. "Behave yourself. *Back!*"

"When does she start obeying?" Pop asked.

"Haru, give her that beer!" I ordered.

16

"When senseless boy leaves Terror of Crocodiles alone as his mother wishes."

Oh, the snake! His eyes glistened like a snake's too, and I remembered the circus man warning Lem and me that he was the worst liar, thief, and throat-cutter this side of Bombay.

The trees were beginning to bend and Pop said, "Better slide off, son."

"Quick, dear!" Mother screamed. "Slip off behind, but be careful!"

"Dot, set me down!" I said firmly. Until now she had never failed me, but now her one idea was that drink. The trees were groaning. Dot let out a bellow that had a new sound in it. She was growing angry, and that scared me. "Haru, give her the beer *instantly!*"

"When silly boy promises . . ."

That was too much for Pop. He pushed Haru back with the palm of his hand, picked up the pail, and carried it right up to angry Dot. He had his nerve with him, for he didn't know how she would act, she was so irritated. He held up the pail and she sank her trunk into it with a *whish-whush* of bubbly satisfaction that splattered root beer all over his face. But Pop didn't say a word, and Dot sucked up the beer, and it made the same sound as when you are sucking soda through a straw and trying not to waste any, only a hundred times louder.

Pop set down the empty pail and began swabbing his face, but his brow was smooth as a bathtub, and I could see that Haru had done me a kindness. For holding that

17

pail for Dot while she satisfied her thirst had converted Pop to elephants. It was like when he had fed a stray dog at the backdoor, and got fond of her, and he still has Blinky. I wished there'd been an extra pail for Mother to hold, for she was nervous.

When I looked around Lem was approaching and Haru had disappeared. The moment I finished introducing Lem, Mother said, "This performance settles it. I wish you had seen it. I wouldn't have a night's sleep if I left our son in camp with this monster." She told Lem about it, and then said to Pop, "If you will go tell Mr. Wieldy that we are withdrawing him, I'll go help him pack."

"Now, Mother!" Pop said. "Not so fast."

"But I can't leave, Mother!" I felt as if I'd been struck by lightning. "I love this place."

"You're very changeable," Mother said. "A week ago we could hardly induce you to come."

"Who's changeable?" I asked. "You were set on making me come, and now when I like it, you want to take me away."

"I didn't know it was infested with elephants," Mother said.

"If I go, Dot goes," I told her.

Then Lem spoke up. "Yes, we should insist on that, Mrs. Keets."

"And that settles *that!*" Pop said, with a wink at me that made me feel good. "Where would we keep an elephant?"

"We are leaving the elephant," Mother said firmly.

"Excuse me, ma'am," Lem cut in again. "We cannot be responsible for your son's pet if he leaves."

"We are donating the elephant," Mother said.

"Hardly," Pop said drily. "You don't understand, Mother. Dot's worth money. We can't afford to throw money away. Besides, you heard Mr. Higgity. If the boy goes, the elephant goes. Can you drive an elephant?"

"Don't be absurd!" Mother said.

"One other thing. Whose elephant is it?" Pop asked.

"What has that got to do with it?" Mother demanded.

"Everything," Pop said, and did that make me happy!

But as usual I got happy too soon, for Pop went on, "It's the boy's elephant. He's invested in a nice property, and he's got several weeks to find a buyer. He knows I can't afford to keep an elephant and I don't propose to be saddled with one." Then he turned to me. "My advice is to get in touch with all the zoos, circuses, and animal brokers there are. If you can't sell her in a month, then rent her out, or give her away. You can't bring her home."

Lem nodded agreement and said, "We agree to support Dot through the season, but of course she reverts to her owner thereafter."

"The situation is now clear," Pop said. "If you can't arrange a businesslike settlement by the middle of August, I shall be obliged to take a hand. Is that satisfactory?"

I couldn't talk. I was all choked up at the thought of losing Dot. Pop repeated the question and I shook my

19

head. "How would you like it if I asked you to get rid of Blinky?"

"It doesn't cost me $30 a day to feed her," Pop said. "Now we must shove off."

He said goodbye to Lem and I saw them to the car. It sure was a narrow escape.

CHAPTER III

Blis was waiting for me, for he had run into Haru and had heard what happened. Blis is the opposite of most boys, for he does think of somebody else but himself part of the time. He knew at once that Haru's acting up was serious for me, and for the camp. He saw, too, that I was boiling mad.

"The snake!" I exclaimed. "That's gratitude! We save him from Sheriff Wickendorf! We overlook the fact that he was kidnapping Dot. And then he turns on me, in front of Mother, and almost gets me taken away from camp. I've a mind to shove him back into Hoggset jail."

"You're angry," Blis said. "We've got to consider this very carefully, when you cool off."

"I'll not cool very fast with him here."

"Now look," and Blis stopped in the trail to my tent. "Haru's dangerous. He's the kind you don't know is

21

loaded until he goes off and there are a couple of funerals."

"That's why I'd better hand him over to Wickendorf." It made me feel blown up and big to say so.

"It would be the greatest risk we could take," Blis said calmly. "We mustn't let him out of our sight."

"Suppose he trains Dot to disobey me and hate me?"

"So that's what's at the bottom of it!"

"What do you mean by that?"

"Jealousy. Mutual jealousy," Blis said slowly. "Haru's jealous of you because Dot likes you, and you're jealous of Haru because he's had Dot's affection from the first. This is bad." Blis studied me quietly, the way he studies something he is going to draw, and it's like a compliment.

"I'm not jealous," I said, but I wondered if I was.

"One thing," Blis said seriously. "You must never, never show it. Don't let Haru even guess it. In fact, if I were you, I'd stay away from Dot for a few days."

"You mean not even see her?" I couldn't believe what I heard.

Blis nodded. "Keep scarce. Don't show that you care a whoop. Let intellect triumph, just once, over what you'd like to do."

I began to heat up again. I thought Blis would take my side better than that. But no. It was me—I, I mean—who had to stay away from Dot! Blis could stand there, watching me, and remain calm and cool because Dot wasn't his elephant, and he wasn't giving up anything. Sometimes I get very tired of brains.

22

"You know I can't do that," I said.

"It's just a suggestion," Blis said. "Now you'd better go up and get acquainted with your boys."

"My boys!" Then I remembered I was a junior counselor and so I was in charge of a tent. "Who'd I draw?"

"You'll see," Blis said with a laugh I didn't like very much and left me. But he stopped once and said, "Do I have to suggest that you keep this strictly under your hat, Keetsie? It's fortunate no one was there, for it's dynamite, and if I'm any judge, Gil Combs knows how to use dynamite . . . Be seeing you."

I passed a tent that kids were swarming in and out of and shrieking around in all stages of insanity. It was my first glimpse of a junior counselor's job and I thought maybe I'd been impulsive again. To want to be one, I mean. Whosever tent it was didn't know an awful lot about keeping order. I went back and glanced in and I saw it was Gil Combs' tent. I hadn't realized he would be a junior counselor, too, but I didn't feel too bad about it. He was shouting to some kid to shut up and didn't see me.

When I reached Murdo's and my tent I saw that someone had pinned *No. 5* on the flap. Then it came over me that I wasn't tenting with him any more. That was another jolt, for Murdo was like a side of me that I didn't know and wanted to find out. There was lots of him I wanted to find out, too. It was like Silas said, Murdo was a woods and you didn't know everything in a woods.

23

The minute I looked in the tent, they deafened me with questions.

"You our tent-master?"

"It's your elephant, isn't it?"

"Can I have first ride?"

"How do you make a cot stand up?"

"Where can I put this?" It was a ukelele.

"Under the piano," snapped a tall skinny guy.

"What'll we name our tent?" asked a red-head who looked like a live wire.

"Sprigg says butterflies spin raccoons, do they?" asked the youngest boy, who was around ten.

"If you want me, I'll be in my knapsack," said the fellow who couldn't make his cot stand up.

Well, I could count, and did, and what had sounded like a mob turned out to be five, and one of them hadn't said a word. He already had slapped everything into shape, and now he lifted the tent flap and left.

"Who's he?" I asked.

"Rugg," the red-head said. "Nobody knows about him. He just disappears."

"He's probably a communist spy," the tall, skinny fellow said.

"I'm Dempsy," the red-head said. "He's Forman," pointing to the skinny boy. "He's Sprigg," who still held the ukelele. "And he's Taddie," pointing to the youngster. "If you watch him long enough, you can tell he's moving."

24

"But you find out he doesn't move *anywhere*," Forman said. I could tell he was a sour one.

"Stop riding the kid," Sprigg said to Forman. "You could help him once in a while."

"So I could," Forman said sarcastically. "Like you could stop offering advice. Why don't you help him?"

"Let's decide what to name our tent," Taddie said. He had paid no attention to the remarks about him. He was examining a mosquito bite on his leg.

"What's the rush? Let's get the tent straightened up first," I said. But they explained that Lem Higgity would be around to collect the tent names. He was going to read them at Council Fire and we would vote which was the funniest or fittest and the winning tent drew a chocolate cake and cokes.

"Elephant Tent. That's what I call it, anyway," Taddie said. I could tell that he was going to be determined.

"Ant Heap. Look at it," Forman said.

"That's no name," Dempsy said.

I saw there would soon be a fight and that I might as well start in being a junior counselor right off. So I said that we'd choose the name after we got the tent in order, and each fellow must think hard, for we wanted that chocolate cake.

That next half hour was a work-out. By the time we'd got the cots made, clothes hung on hooks, the stuff we didn't need stored in dufflebags, the toothbrushes separated from the shoes and towels, the toothpaste scraped off comic books, and the floor swept, I felt like a five-star general.

It was funny how soon the fellows stood out from each other. Forman called Taddie "Fallen Arches" because he was so slow. But I found that Taddie could move fast when he wanted. His trouble was his interest in little things. Everything was new and he had to examine it. Forman was easy—he was the tent gripe. His conceit suffered from overweight. Sprigg was the tent advisor, but he had a sense of humor. Dempsy had a trouble you felt ashamed to find fault with—he was just too helpful. I was afraid he'd soon be asking if he could brush my teeth for me.

Picking the tent name was like sledding uphill. Each fellow voted for his own choice. Dempsy gave in first, to be helpful, and Forman finally had his way and we called it "Ant Heap." I thought he had something at that.

"Daybreak at last!" Sprigg announced. "The sun rose from the sea with flamingo-touched fingers."

"Choke him!" Forman said. "Cut him into fifths and feed him to the fishes."

"Allow me to review the new camp policy!" Sprigg said. "Build campers . . . Live dangerously . . . Lynch Forman." He set about carrying out the policy by tackling the gripe. They went to the floor and thrashed around. Their long legs sideswiped most of the cots. Dempsy and I tried to separate them. Taddie stood on the wreckage and cheered for Sprigg.

That was the moment Lem Higgity chose to show

up. No junior counselor could ever look feebler and sillier. But all Lem said was, "All right, boys. Get busy and straighten up. This tent has to pass inspection before you swim. Where's Rugg?"

I had to confess that I didn't know, and still Lem didn't bawl me out. He sure knew how to make you a friend of his. He handed me a typed list of rules for tent order. They called for tent inspection by the junior counselor daily, and by the brass on Saturday mornings. Marks would be given and a weekly prize to the best tent. Also a summer's prize at the end. That's why we needed tent names. "Have you chosen yours yet?" Lem asked.

"Ant Heap," Forman said.

"Elephant Tent," Taddie contradicted hopefully. He sure was a persistent little cuss.

"Ant Heap got the vote," I told Lem and he wrote it down.

"Now can we go see the elephant?" Taddie asked.

"What did Mr. Pickerel say about that?" Lem said to Taddie.

"He said after supper."

"So after supper it is."

"But our tent-master *owns* the elephant," Taddie persisted. "He can tell Mr. Pickerel when *he* can see her."

"Keets will explain to you about that," Lem said kindly. Then he gave my boys a talk on tent neatness and clothes and hygiene and sanitation, and they listened. I tried to study out how it was he made them listen so

27

quietly and easily. But before I had fixed on any one thing, he quit and beckoned me outside.

We walked down the trail, out of hearing of anyone, and I supposed he was going to read me a lecture on keeping order. But it was Haru that was on his mind.

"I've been talking to him about his unintelligent conduct before your parents," Lem said. "And he's trying to put the squeeze on me."

"How's that?" I asked.

"He says he can't control Dot if you keep spoiling her."

"How do I spoil her? He's crazy." Then I thought of Blis and said, "He's just jealous, that's the trouble."

"Yes, you're right," Lem said. "Dot is fond of you and shows it and Haru is jealous. But he knows, unfortunately, that he is essential to this camp. We have to be able to tell parents that we employ a professional elephant keeper, or they would react the way your mother did, and want to take their darlings away. So that's how Haru can throw his weight around more than I like. Mr. Wieldy and I were wondering if you'd be willing to . . . well, you know, sort of play along with the situation for a few days, Keetsie."

"Sure," I said, but I felt kind of sickish because I could tell Lem was trying to break some bad news to me. "How do you mean?"

Lem's chin stiffened, like he needed all his will, and he said, "Perhaps you'd agree to let Haru take full charge

28

of Dot for a day or two and . . . you know, keep in the background."

I felt a black storm rising inside me. The next day or two was when I wanted to be with Dot especially. I wanted to show her off and take my tent rides. It wasn't fair.

"I know what you're thinking," Lem said. "And I don't blame you, Keetsie boy. Asking this favor is the hardest thing I've had to do. I wouldn't ask it if I could think of an alternative. We can't get another keeper. I've tried talking to Haru, and you know what that's like."

"Were you talking to Blis?" I asked.

"No. Why?" Lem was surprised.

"He said the same thing, Lem. He said we were both jealous, and I must keep it dark, and the best way was to stay away from Dot."

"Thanks for telling me," Lem said.

The way he said that made me sure I'd do what he wanted. "How long do you think I'd have to . . . to give Dot up?" I asked.

"That's the question that bothers us most," Lem said, and it showed how square-shooting he was, not to let me off easy with a nice answer. "As I dope it out, when we settle down into a routine, and Haru sees that you can take Dot or leave her, he'll be less afraid that you want to separate him from Dot. Then I can have another talk with him. Will you trust to my judgment as to how long?

29

I said a day or two, but it might have to be a week? Is that possible?"

I nodded, for there wasn't anything else to do with Lem asking that way.

He rested his hand on my shoulder. "I told Mr. Wieldy you'd help us, Keetsie. Don't forget, we're all for you —after the camp. And we won't forget this, boy. Now, get your kids into their swim things and bring them down for tests. Then Council's at five. I know you won't mention any of this."

"Can I tell Blis?"

"Of course, Blis. The thing is to be your good-humored natural self. You'll be plenty occupied with your boys. And when they come up this evening to see Dot get her supper, you come, too, if you can take it." Then Lem shook my hand and left, and I knew I was going to take it.

CHAPTER IV

Lem was correct about my being occupied. I found my tent fighting for first ride on the elephant. Taddie had pulled the blankets off Sprigg's cot because Sprigg had told him littlest went last. So Sprigg was chasing Taddie around behind the other cots. Taddie was showing he could be fast, slippery, and cagey. Dempsy was trying to help. He had grabbed Sprigg's ukelele and was going to bat Sprigg over the head, but Forman held his arm.

"Give it to me! Give it here!" Forman was saying.

Taddie slithered underneath Forman's cot to escape Sprigg. Sprigg upset the cot to get Taddie. Forman succeeded in wrenching the uke from Dempsy and yelled, "Bash their heads in! It's the quickest way." Dempsy jumped at Forman, and I held Forman's arm to prevent the uke from being smashed.

31

Taddie caught sight of me and jumped at me shouting, "Can't I ride first? Can't I?"

I knew that if Lem saw this unruly mess now, he'd decide I wasn't junior counselor material.

"Nobody rides for a week if this mess isn't cleaned up in ten minutes!" I shouted. "Give me this," and I took the

uke from Forman forcibly. "Dempsy, help Taddie put up his cot. Sprigg, get busy on yours. Forman, help me with Rugg's."

They weren't half as surprised as I was to hear me ordering them around. I guess it was because I was so low that nothing much mattered. They didn't exactly quail before me, like they would if I'd been Murdo, and he was mad, but they jumped to it. I was mighty thankful they didn't know I wasn't master of my own elephant. Blis and Lem had been right about keeping that dark. That was one secret I would never let out.

"Now can I?" Taddie said. "Can I ride Dot first?"

"Drown him," Forman advised. "It's painless and he's insured."

"All out for the swim!" I shouted. "Place clothes on cot. We all go together."

They shed shirts, pants, and shoes as if they were burning. Dempsy had his shorts on before Taddie had comfortably sat down to take off his sneakers.

"He'll be ready for tomorrow's swim," Forman said. "Let's go."

"We all go together," I repeated.

"Let's help him," Dempsy said. Sprigg jumped to the other side. They had the kid stripped before he could yell. Forman held his shorts. Dempsy and Sprigg lifted him and dropped him into them. Forman pushed him out of the tent. Dempsy and Sprigg took a hand apiece and ran him down the trail. Mr. Pickerel couldn't have organized it better.

As it was Mr. Pickerel had the swim tests organized to the last splash. He had made out charts for the junior counselors to mark, and we ran the kids through like a conveyor belt.

"Pile the drowned ones in the tub," Forman said. He was full of neat ideas like that.

"Does he always talk like a shark with bad teeth?" Blis asked me.

33

"He has a heart of gold," I said, for I found out that a junior counselor always stood up for his tent. Then I caught sight of Quizzy, our ex-Quiz Kid, and authority on space, and called him over so I could find out what happened to the rest of us six Originals. Quizzy was in Blister's tent. Downy was in Murdo's. Gil Combs had nabbed Stringy so they could talk baseball all night. Gil was a junior counselor, of course, and it turned out he was a star pitcher for Laidlow High, some place in Florida.

The more I heard about Gil, the more scared I got. He was big, which gets boys, though I was almost his size. But it was his quiet way that scared me. He was like a rock that don't have to go around shouting "I'm a rock." It just sits there until you stub your foot on it, and that's the way Gil acted. I'd heard enough to know that Mr. Pickerel considered him a wonder. Then Lem was mighty appreciative of him for having brought the boys, even if my Dot started it. And now Stringy was shining up to him, and Haru practically fell on his face when Gil walked by. Maybe I was getting another case of jealousy, but I sure wasn't going to show it to Blis or Lem.

With the tests over, the boys swam. It was fun watching Murdo. Some boys were picking on a misfit in Murdo's tent they called Glurpy, and he looked like it. I watched Murdo do the crawl on a rescue mission. Being made a junior counselor had changed him a lot in four hours. I remembered what Lem had told me, when

34

I thought Murdo was washed up. Lem said that all Murdo needed was a little responsibility and he'd be a prince. And now he was one, only slightly pigheaded.

After he'd saved Glurpy's life, he came back to the dock and sat by me. "How you doing with your junior counseling?" he asked.

"It's kind of like making a lot of eels sit up straight," I said. "But I've got a swell bunch."

"So've I," Murdo said, panting. "Take even Glurpy there. He's probably got something to him, and I'm going to find out what it is."

"They all have, I guess," I said.

"They want to know who gets first ride on Dot," Murdo said. "Have you doped out a plan?"

"Mr. Pickerel's organizing it," I said.

"Say, Lem had better watch that man or he'll have this camp organized into a steamroller. What's he got to do with Dot? She's still your property."

I wished I could tell Murdo, because he would have been as sore in my favor as I was. Most fellows overlook what happens to other fellows. You tell them your leg has to be amputated, and they're mighty sympathetic for about a minute. "Gosh, that's bad," they say. "I run a splinter into my finger, too. Look at it," and they hold up their finger and forget your leg. But Murdo isn't like that.

I might have let on, in spite of myself, how things lay, but the coming-out whistle blew and the new boys were sent up to write a letter home telling why they were at

35

Camp Chesunquoik. Mr. Pickerel had mimeographed a specimen letter as guidance. It sure was full of helpful hints. It mentioned twenty or thirty nice things to say about camp, and it sounded wonderfully hopeful about our baseball team seeing as we hadn't even a diamond yet. It worked Dot in mighty tactfully, by describing our professional elephant-keeper before it got to Dot, so every parent wouldn't pass out with the shock. There were a couple of remarks about Nature's handiwork which didn't sound like they came from boys. But in general it was pretty useful and didn't take more than ten minutes to copy.

I would have been late to Council if Dempsy hadn't offered to help Taddie along up the trail. Taddie wanted to count the midges in a cloud. Then he tried to get two spiders to race. And finally he bet himself that he couldn't pile six stones on top of each other and wanted to see who won. I never knew a boy so interested in things at the wrong time.

Lem hadn't called Council when I reached the bungalow, but all of us counselors were there. Gil Combs was showing Stringy how he pitched a curve, and we all looked on. It didn't rattle Gil to have so many admirers. I don't think he knew we were there.

"It's all in not snapping your wrist too late," Gil said to Stringy. "Big Wham Belson showed me."

"You know the Big Wham?" Stringy asked.

"Many of the big leaguers train near our place," Gil explained. "Mase asks them over to see the tigers and they give me pointers. See, you twist your whole arm to throw a curve, and you ease into the twist as your arm comes up even with your ear. This way."

Gil was right about getting his whole arm into it. He worked in his shoulder, elbow, and wrist, not to mention hips, knee-joints, and little toe. He looked like a serious boa constrictor having a fit. Yet there wasn't anything show-offy about him. I could see that Stringy knew he was in luck to have a pitcher that Big Wham Belson had trained.

Stringy noticed me watching and beckoned me over. "Keetsie's going to try out for short," he said to Gil. "Tell him what you told me about playing the position."

"Gladly," Gil said. "Have you seen Spurt Hennissy play short?" he asked.

"No. I've never watched many pro games."

"Do you know Spurt, too?" asked Stringy and he was more impressed than ever.

"Oh yes, he comes over to study Mase's twin kangaroos. He says they can teach him how to get the jump on the ball." Gil turned to me. "The main thing is, Keets, you've got to cover ground like an antelope."

"I've never seen one," I said.

"We have a small herd," Gil said modestly. "When we take Dot home, I can show you how they run."

Just then Lem looked out of the Bungalow door and said, "All right, fellows," and that kept me from blowing up, but all through the meeting, Gil's words kept coming back. "When we take Dot home." I don't be-

37

lieve Murdo heard them, or he would have flared up like a torch.

Lem and Mr. Pickerel sat side by side at the end of the table and looked as efficient as a pair of scissors. Blis, I, Murdo, Gil, and two other fellows from the deceased camp sat around the rest of the table facing them. Lem had a list of things to discuss as long as a train, but he was experienced at pushing things through, and Mr. Pickerel cleaned up after him like a windshield wiper. We set up a rotating work program to help Silas—table-setters, clean-up gang, and so forth. We appointed Council Fire-makers, canoe-repairers, and a crew to make the baseball diamond.

Murdo asked who was listed to wash his hands, because he was fussy about that. Mr. Pickerel said that whoever it was they couldn't begin too soon. You could always trust Mr. Pickerel to have a comeback.

Murdo didn't fancy having a camp magazine either, when Mr. Pickerel brought that up. "What the heck! Buy 'em comics." Murdo snorted.

"It's for home consumption," Mr. Pickerel explained. "We don't want parents barging in to find out what Sammy's doing. And the boys like it because it saves letter writing."

"It's too much like school for me," Murdo complained. "I thought camp was for doing what you want."

"You'd be bored in a week," Mr. Pickerel retorted. "Nothing leads so quickly to dissatisfaction."

38

"As fun?" Murdo asked. "That's a new one. That's like saying that nothing makes you so unhappy as being in a good humor. I don't get it. Don't you like loafing? Lying in the sun and being lazy, and going in for a swim when you get hot, and coming out and throwing the bull around a bit? That's camping for me. Baseball, sure, and trips. We'll put them across and like it. But in-between we don't want every minute organized to heck like a pinball game where you have to run down a certain groove to ring the bell."

"Write it up for the magazine," Mr. Pickerel said and smiled.

Lem saw Murdo getting dark around the eyes and saw it was time to stop the duel. "We all agree with you, Murdo. Camp's for fun. It's for enjoying yourself, competing in order to improve, making friends, getting new insights, and fitting into nature. Being intelligently relaxed, as you say, is the basis of everything else. Some of the youngsters have to be led, and some will gripe, and that's one advantage of the magazine. It can show what's been fun, and the fun coming up, and also it gives the gripers a place to buzz off. Has anyone a name for our magazine?"

"You named it," Gil said. "The Buzz-off." Everyone laughed.

"Not bad," Lem grinned. "The Chesunquoik Buzz. How many approve?"

We liked that. Then Stringy suggested a baseball game

with Hoggset and Lem agreed to take it up with the town. We put through some more business, and Silas's bugle went for supper.

Before the meeting broke up, Lem cleared his throat and said, "One more little matter which is not to go beyond these walls. As some of you may know, Dot caused a little apprehension this afternoon by not obeying an order. She has been well trained. But a little period of reconditioning is called for. So Keets has very thoughtfully turned her back into Haru's hands for a week or so at considerable sacrifice, for he is actually Dot's owner and master and naturally relinquishes the pleasure of doing the honors with regret. Haru, of course, resents the events of this morning. I refer to Murdo's invaluable act of overtaking Haru and bringing him back. It seems to me that this camp owes much to Murdo, to Gil for discovering us, and to Keets for his unique addition to our camp life. Mr. Wieldy has asked me to express his appreciation of these services."

Gil spoke up the minute Lem finished. "I'll look after Haru, sir. I've done a little towards cooling him off. We're on excellent terms. I wish you'd let me take full responsibility for him."

Mr. Pickerel butted right in and said, "Gil could do it, too. He has a way of getting what he wants."

"The heck with . . ." Murdo began, but Blis interrupted.

"Dot is now an essential member of this camp. That makes a good keeper essential. Haru is on the temperamental side. He is not kindly disposed to Murdo or to Keets at this time for obvious reasons. But Gil is a neutral. If Gil can keep Haru sweet, I vote that he should be allowed to try, but with full understanding, of course, of Keets' rights in the matter."

"Why you Judas . . ." Murdo muttered.

"I'd like to hear what Keets has to say," Lem declared.

He looked at me and I knew what he wanted me to say so I said, "I agree."

"Well, I'm nuts, or you're a cockeyed potato," Murdo muttered.

"Council dismissed," Lem said.

CHAPTER V

Murdo did not leave the Bungalow. Instead he leaned across me to say to Blis, "What's the idea of handing over Keetsie's control of Haru to this big blow from Florida?"

"Turn off the alarm," Blis said. "Keets understands the maneuver. Lem and I have his interests at heart as much as you do. And Gil isn't a big blow. He's much more dangerous. He's so used to getting what he wants that he can imagine no other conclusion to a matter. You just can't knock him down and call it a day, for he'll get right up again. We have to go into this situation carefully. Meanwhile Keets is right in lying low and letting Gil think things are going his way. Now please don't spoil it by barging in like a bull moose at a chess game."

A week before Murdo wouldn't have let Blis talk to him like that. He'd have got sore and blood would have flowed in the gutter. But he paused to think these facts over, and Silas bugled again, and that was that.

We found menus written in green ink on birchbark on the tables. Downy, who headed the supper squad, had done the work. This is what we read:

SILAS BROADBEAM'S FEAST OF WELCOME TO CAMP CHESUNQUOIK

Porcupine Soup

Roast Strutter	Bog Blood
Stuffed Breadfruit	Baked Moles

Creamed Bullets
Abyssinian Delirium
Liquidation.

Lem made a speech of acceptance before the squad started carrying in the blood and bullets and so forth. He said that he couldn't make head or tail of the menu, and he certainly wasn't going to eat strange dishes like that sight unseen. But the camp was lucky to have an ex-Quiz Kid among its guests, and Quizzy would interpret the menu for us.

Well, that was a stumper. Quizzy was as surprised by the request as by the funny names. Silas came in to answer questions. Quizzy guessed every one of them but the Abyssinian Delirium. Black bean soup spiked with lemon juice . . . Roast turkey . . . Cranberry sauce . . . Baked sweet potatoes . . . Hot rolls with butter inside . . . Creamed peas . . . and the Liquidation was milk or iced tea. Abyssinia was where Silas's only colored ancestor came from and the delirium was an understate-

43

ment, for this dessert was macaroons slabbed onto ice cream with butterscotch sauce poured onto it. Murdo said it ought to be called Fly-paper Special, and it sure did stick.

Lem announced that anyone who had strength enough left to reach the stockade could see Dot have her supper. No one was to enter the stockade unless Haru invited him.

The last thing I wanted was to watch Haru gloat over his keeping me from my elephant, but I knew I had to. Taddie took my hand. Blis passed us and said, "This is the acid test, fellow."

"What's that?" Taddie asked.

"A little joke we have."

"Why aren't you laughing then, if it's a joke?"

Dempsy joined us. "Can I help you feed Dot?" he asked.

"I'm letting my servant do the work," I told him.

After about forty more questions we reached the stockade. Taddie took one look at Dot and said, "Is that all the bigger she is?" It just shows that you can't suit everybody, and I guess Nature has stopped trying, or there wouldn't be ants and mosquitoes.

Dot was all steamed up with pride at having such a circle of admirers. She swayed and made comfortable noises. Haru hid an apple under his armpit and Dot searched him. She knew where it was but pretended it was everywhere else. Her little red eyes twinkled when she blew down his blouse or tickled his neck. Finally she wrapped her trunk about Haru's chest, lifted him off the ground, and shook him until he let the apple fall. She dropped him with a squeal, picked up the apple and threw it high over her back. She almost caught it, too.

"Where are you playing her, Stringy?" Gil called.

"Not catcher anyway." And everybody laughed.

"Backstop!" Murdo said. "Dot'd make a good backstop."

Haru looked over at Gil and said, "Does Worthy Master wish to feed his Necklace of Beauty?"

I felt hot right up into my hair. I saw the boys glancing at me as Gil squeezed himself into the stockade and Haru handed him a bucket of raw vegetables. More and more boys sneaked glances at me. I knew what they were wondering after being told all day that Dot was my elephant.

"Why aren't you in there doing that?" a voice asked sarcastically, and I saw it was Forman.

"Gil wanted to do it tonight," I said.

"Why's he call Gil Worthy Master if you are?" Taddie asked.

"Can I feed her tomorrow?" Dempsy asked.

"We'll see. Maybe in a week or so," I said.

I stuck it out until the bugle went for Council Fire, but I didn't fool the boys. They went polite on me, and that's awful. The minute fellows go polite like that, you don't know what they're thinking, but it is sure to be the opposite. The only thing to do is to stop it right then and there. But I didn't know how to.

45

Blis walked down to the fire with me. "You put it over," he said.

"I did not. Forman thinks I'm a fourflusher. Every kid in my tent will think I'm a pushover. I can tell."

"Keep your shirt on," Blis said. "Play sly for a few days and we'll detour out of this jam."

The Council Fire squad had piled a whale of a lot of wood, and it was beautiful out there on the point in the twilight. Nobody talked much. Lem asked Taddie and Quizzy to come forward, and he took them behind the pile.

"What's up?" Dempsy asked. "Do you think they want help?"

"It's just the annual initiation," Forman said languidly. "They cut the throats of the two youngest boys as a sacrifice. It brings good luck."

"Pity you're not the youngest," Sprigg said, and everyone laughed.

In the dusk Taddie and Quizzy carried two birchbark torches that had been kindled. They met and touched flames, then held the united flame to the pile. The fire jumped as if it had been waiting.

"Fire—enthusiasm," Lem said. "We unite to do things better."

We watched the growing fire spiral and swirl into the sky. Presently Lem read the tent names: Monkey House . . . Spaceship . . . First Base . . . Ant Heap . . . Elephant . . . Mystery . . . Aquarium . . . Higgity

Hall. Spaceship got the most votes. I knew that was Blis's tent for Quizzy had suggested the name. Mystery was Murdo's tent. First Base was Gil's. Aquarium was Mr. Pickerel's. Monkey House and Elephant were tents with counselor's from the other camp. Ant Heap didn't get many votes. I guess the fellows didn't have Forman's sense of humor.

Lem asked Stringy to come forward and talk up baseball, and he was good. He was so full of baseball that the words just came out. He got us so excited about our coming victory over Hoggset that we could hardly wait till morning to lay out the diamond.

By now it was deep dark and the stars shone all over the sky like lanterns. Sprigg said they were strung around like that because the universe was giving a party.

"With Quizzy's permission," Blis said, because Quizzy knew the universe from top to bottom, but nobody saw the point.

A lonesome sound rose from the darkest black of the wilderness across the lake. It went *who—whooooo—WHOOOOOooooo*—and gave you the shivers. I wondered if Asa Lirrup, who lived over there in Little Yellowstone with his mother, could have invented it, like his moose-call.

"What's that?" Taddie asked.

"Nothing to be afraid of," Murdo said. "It's just a blood-suckeroo. They're no bigger than an ostrich. They settle on your face when you're asleep and spread their

47

feathers so you can't scream. But they don't take more than a quart of blood and you hardly feel it, except for being a little light-headed next morning."

"You must've been a victim," Gil said and a couple of his friends snickered, but most were listening in case it came nearer. Sure enough, it went again *who—whooooo —WHOOOOOOooooo*—much nearer and the blood chilled down my back like it was off a glacier.

"I hate to contradict an authority like Murdo," Lem said quietly. "But that bird is the great barred owl. He's starting his nightly hunt for mice and other small mammals. So our sleep will be undisturbed, and Murdo will have to give another reason for being light-headed."

We all laughed when suddenly we were startled by the owl going off right in the middle of camp. It was Silas answering the big barred one on his bugle, and he made it sound mighty wild and owly. He didn't fool the real owl, though, for he shut up.

So Silas quit owl-talk and played Taps, the soldiers' goodnight. It brought back the night Murdo had run off to the circus. It was very sad, like he was saying goodnight to everything. It made you think of going down a long dark tunnel without any end, all by yourself, with only the wilderness around. I let my knee touch Blis's to be sure it wasn't so, and he didn't draw away. Maybe he needed company too.

After the last clear note went out into the loneliness, Lem dismissed us. He said he wanted all the tent lanterns out in twenty minutes. It sure had been a big day, and I guessed everyone would be dog tired, but I guessed wrong. When I reached the tent they were scrapping already.

"Ant Heap's a lousy name," Sprigg said to Forman. "Now we don't get any chocolate cake and I'm hungry."

"Why don't you move?" Forman suggested.

"You'll move before I do," Sprigg said.

"My shoe's in a knot," Taddie announced.

"I thought Dot was your elephant," Forman said to me.

"Give it a rest," Dempsy said to Forman.

"So she is his elephant," Sprigg said.

"How come Haru calls Gil his Worthy Master?" Forman asked.

"My shoe's in a worse knot," Taddie moaned.

"Here," Dempsy went over to help.

"Let's hustle into bed so this tent doesn't get marked down," I said.

"I asked you a question," Forman said to me. "Are you running the elephant or is that dim-face saying who gets the rides?"

"I'm running this tent and saying who gets to bed, Forman," I told him.

"It's too tight, it won't come off," Taddie said.

"Quit hedging," Forman said angrily, "or I'll feel like pasting you one."

I wondered what a junior counselor did in a jam like this, but there was no time to think. "All right," I said and stood so close in front of him that I could look straight into his eyes. "Try it. Paste me one." I didn't even make a fist.

Sprigg came a step closer and Dempsy straightened up. Forman passed. I guess he wasn't mad enough, or else he saw he'd have to take on all three of us. Anyhow he said, "That's answer enough for me," and turned away.

"All right, fellows," I said to Sprigg and Dempsy. "Let's hit the hay."

Rugg poked his head in and said, "How do you attract owls?"

"I'm putting this lantern out in six minutes," I warned him.

"All right by me," mystery-boy Rugg said. "I'll be asleep in five."

He was, too, but I was feeling too good to sleep. It was on account of Forman. I was a junior counselor with one notch on my gun. Pop would have been surprised. I wondered what he had done to grow into a man.

CHAPTER VI

When it came to getting things done, the team of Higgity and Pickerel was tops. Breakfast hadn't been over twenty minutes next morning before they had the dining-tent squad, the blanket-airing checkers, the baseball diamond construction gang, the Chesunquoik Buzz staff, and the additional latrine-diggers all shoving ahead at full blast.

Mr. Pickerel strolled around from one bunch to another as happy as ants at a picnic. He kept telling the boys to go easy, because camp wasn't school or anything, and nobody was making them work, and he didn't want them to wear themselves out, and pleasant remarks like that, until they fairly ran with sweat to show him they didn't have to. Silas could hardly admire Mr. Pickerel enough, and said it was a pity the country didn't hold to slavery still on account of what a grand slave-driver was lost in him. There wasn't anything the boys wouldn't do for him, except quit working.

Lem took me away from a canoe-calking job to say, "Did you notice a howdah being auctioned off at Hoggset the day you got Dot?"

"A howdah? What's that?"

"It's the thing you ride in on top of an elephant. Haru said Dot wore one in the parades, but he doesn't know what became of it."

"I doubt if those farmers would've got stuck with a howdah," I told Lem. "It's probably kicking around Hoggset."

"I think so myself," Lem said. "I'm taking Stringy to Hoggset to rig up a ball game, and Gil to look them over if they're playing, and I think I'll take Haru to see if the howdah's worth buying. Mr. Wieldy suggests that you go too. He believes in fellows getting together, you know. How about it?"

I thought I'd be more at home with a couple of rattle-snakes than Haru and Gil but I said sure, it'd be fun, and so we piled into the truck and headed for town. Stringy was excited at the idea of defending Camp Chesunquoik's baseball title, though he hadn't even a playing field yet, let alone a team.

"Don't be too sure that Hoggset has a team," Lem cautioned.

"Of course it has a team," Stringy said.

"I'm just asking you not to be too sure."

"Maine's in America, isn't it?" Stringy asked.

52

"It is thought to be," Lem said.

"And Hoggset's in Maine?"

"That is almost certain," Lem said.

"Then Hoggset has a ball club," Stringy said. "Any town in America that size that doesn't have a ball club isn't American and ought to be run out of the country."

That made us laugh, but Lem shook his head and said, "You live in America, Stringy?"

"I sure do."

"And you call yourself an American?"

"I sure do," Stringy said again.

"Then how come you don't talk like an American?"

"How don't I?" Stringy asked, for Lem had him puzzled.

"You say these Hoggsetters ought to be run out of the country if they don't suit your way of thinking. Is that American?"

Lem looked around to grin at Stringy because he had him, and the truck plunged into a gulley and nearly broke an axle, and Stringy said, "Is that driving?" And we got a good laugh out of that. Stringy was American enough not to let Lem stump him, anyway.

Haru sat by Gil and I could hear enough, between jolts of the truck, to get pretty hot. Haru's head had been turned, not to say screwed around a couple of times, by Gil's attention, but Lem acted as if he didn't hear a word. I knew it was Camp Policy No. 1 to sweeten Haru up, but it made me sick to hear the plans Gil was laying with Haru. It was all what they'd do the minute they got Dot

53

to Florida, and how pleased Mase would be to have the Master of All Conceivable Elephants, as Gil called Haru now, living on his place. You could see Haru sort of swoon with importance when Gil laid it on. They didn't mind me at all. I was just a kind of spare going for the ride.

Gil was especially set on making Florida sound India-like or better, so Haru'd feel at home there and wouldn't miss the Ganges. I must say the Florida publicity people missed a bet when they didn't hire Gil to talk up the place. He was very good on box turtles and scaly-backed lizards and diamondback rattlesnakes, but he outdid himself on the deadly cottonmouth moccasin snakes in their swamps.

"What's the matter with the Maine swamps?" Lem asked when his native pride couldn't stand it any longer.

"They lack the beautiful mystery," Gil said. "No moss, no alligators waiting for you to step in their mouths, and especially no cottonmouth moccasins."

"How could you bear to leave?" I asked.

Gil opened his mouth seriously to tell me, but the truck jounced into a ravine in the road that they'd call a canyon out West and Gil nearly bit his tongue off. I wondered if Lem had done it on purpose. At any rate we didn't hear any more about Florida and presently we were passing a sign saying, "You are now entering the town of Hoggset."

Main Street looked deserted. "Why, the town's dead!" Gil exclaimed.

"Don't you let a Hoggsetter hear you say that," Lem

54

cautioned. "They've the livest sheriff in New England."

Lem drove up to a filling station and a lady was tending it. When Lem asked where everybody was, she said, "At the ball grounds naturally, watching the team practice. Hoggset's in second place in the Poison Ivy League and we'll cop first place by August."

"See?" Stringy said to Lem. "I told you we were in America."

The ball grounds turned out to be the big lot where the circus had passed out and I'd picked up Dot. There was a grandstand and a scoreboard and lots of people standing around watching the practice. Lem drove in not too far from home plate so Gil and Stringy could study their style. They looked pretty terrific to me. Poison Ivy was right. The pitcher was fast. You saw him wind up and you heard the k-plunk in the catcher's mitt, but nothing in between. You knew he was using a ball because the catcher returned it, but that was the only way.

"Not bad," Gil remarked.

Lem looked at Gil but said nothing. We watched until the pitcher had struck out about a dozen men and then Lem said, "Are you sure you want to play this gang, Stringy?"

"Why not?"

"They look pretty fast to me."

"They can't have more than nine men playing at once," Stringy said.

"The pitcher's only got straight stuff," Gil said.

"That's right," Stringy said. "Stand up to him and you've got him. We'll be hitting the guy by the third inning."

When they slacked off to drink out of their bucket, Lem asked who was managing the Hoggset team. "Snag Wickendorf, the pitcher."

"Sheriff Wickendorf's son?" Lem asked.

"That's what they claim." The guy raised his voice and yelled, "Hey, Snag . . . you're wanted."

Snag took his time coming over. His walk was mighty independent. He wasn't old, maybe nineteen, but he hadn't wasted any time toughening up. There wasn't a flaw in him anywhere that way. It was like Lem said later, if they needed a baseball cover, they could take a strip of his hide.

Lem introduced Stringy and told him we were looking for a game. The minute Snag heard we were from Camp Chesunquoik, his neck jerked once like a rooster's and he said, "So you're the guys who gave my old man the runaround. Or don't you remember?"

Lem didn't bat an eye. "Sure we remember. Nobody can forget your father. A most conscientious man."

"Well, isn't this nice!" Snag said out of the corner of his mouth. "We'll take you on. It'll be a pleasure. Say Saturday?"

"Couldn't possibly," Lem said.

"Saturday week?"

"Still too soon to beat you."

"You're not beating us," Snag said. "Saturday fort-night?"

Well, they settled for that and then Lem talked umpire. Snag told him to suit himself—one funeral was as easy to arrange as another. Lem said he knew a good man who'd never been buried yet. By then the players were shouting for Snag, so Lem asked a bystander about the howdah. That puzzled the fellow. He thought Lem was trying to say howdy and not quite making it.

"It's a pavilion that sits on a elephant," Lem explained.

"What elephant?" the man asked.

"Worthy Master's," Haru spoke up and nodded at Gil.

"Mine," I said.

"Camp Chesunquoik has an elephant, and I'm hunting the howdah that goes with it. Haru, will you describe it."

Haru stood up to describe it. "It is wide," and he swept his hands out one way and swooshed them the other. "And high." He hoisted them above his head and then let them flutter. "With curtains." Then he dribbled them down. "And tassels. Very fine howdah." And still the man was too dumb to take it in.

Gil tried next. "Listen," he said to the man, "it's just a sort of open-work elephant balcony in fancy colors. You couldn't mistake it."

"We want to know who bought it at the circus auction," I said.

57

"Oh, auction!" the man snapped. "Why didn't you say so first?" He turned to the good-sized crowd that had collected. "They want that front porch for the elephant that John Pratt couldn't unload on us suckers. Anyone know what became of it?"

Someone remembered that it had been dumped behind the freight station, and there it was. It was kind of imperial looking in spots where it hadn't faded. There was enough gold braid on it to trim a carload of generals. Someone had lifted the bellybands that buckled it around Dot, so Lem bought canvas to make others, and we started home.

Haru was as happy as a giraffe to recover the howdah

and started calling Gil *Sahib* to show his joy. I tried to remember that this sort of thing might go on a week or more and hoped I could take it. I hunted up Blis for company and found him on the back porch of the bungalow with paints and paper and typewriter and stuff all around.

He handed me the cover for the first issue of *The Chesunquoik Buzz*, and it was a honey. It showed a curtain being pulled up by an elephant and revealing a view of our camp lakeside, with boys diving, and Haru performing the Indian rope trick. He had started to type out what he called the Masthead:

Editor-in-Chief	William B. Lister
United Artists	Blis Blister
Proofreader	Taddie
Insulting Remarks, Inc.	Murdo
Chief Cook but not Bottle Washer	Silas Broadbeam, Esq.
Bottle Washer	Asa Lirrup
Board of Critics	Mme. Augustus Lirrup
Other Important Officials	see Camp Directory
Unimportant Officials	consult the above
Chief Convalescent	Hon. Mr. Wieldy

"Asa will feel complimented." I put my finger on his appointment as bottle washer.

"He asked for it," Blis retorted. "Asa came over and we had a long talk about everything. The wash-up squad was running behind Mr. Pickerel's schedule and Asa offered to help out."

"You mean Asa Lirrup would stop inventing to do our dishes?"

"Not as you or I would, Keetsie. Mechanical geniuses don't dabble in dishpans. Asa offered us the use of his geyser. He'd put soap-flakes in the tank instead of Flit and we'd take the dishes over there."

"You know how Mrs. Lirrup would take that!" She was a busy children's librarian all winter and wanted quiet in the summer. She had closed up Camp Chesunquoik I and II and would have closed ours but for Dot. She wouldn't allow a boy on her property, but Blis pretended that she was an amazingly nice and intelligent woman.

"Mrs. Lirrup has revealed still another side of her wonderful nature," Blis said.

"What now? Has she reformed?"

"Women don't reform, Keetsie. They change their minds. Asa tells me that she's laid aside her book on wild animals and plans to do one on boys—as a sequel. She intends to write an exposé of boys."

"It doesn't sound decent. What's she mean?"

"She says that no writer has penetrated our depths and wants to be the first. Like Livingstone in Darkest Africa, you know. She thinks she'll never have as good a chance again to know the worst. So now instead of forbidding Asa to come over here, she is begging him to mingle with us and report what he hears, especially Murdo. It was hearing him trying to drive Dot over her garbage heap that gave her the idea."

"Murdo's a snowdrop compared with Snag Wickendorf. She ought to get a load of him." I told Blis about our morning.

He listened with interest and said, "I took the Haru matter up with Asa, Keetsie. He could see nothing to worry about."

"I thought Asa was intelligent. Here I am in trouble up to my neck, and he can't see anything the matter!"

"Asa asked me to tell you that he'd have your problem solved by 3 p.m. as he had a couple of other things to do first. He wants you to bring Haru over with you."

"That shows he hasn't a notion how bad things are. How can I induce Haru to go anywhere with me, and especially to Little Yellowstone?"

"I suppose he thought you had some initiative," Blis said. "Asa asked me one question I couldn't give him a clear answer to. He wanted to know whether I thought Haru was subhuman, human, or superhuman? I told him I couldn't be sure."

"You don't *know!*" I shouted. "Who's a mouse brain now?"

"You disappoint me, Keetsie. I thought you'd learned not to underrate your companions."

"I suppose you think he's superhuman!" I said bitterly.

"Well, how would you rate yourself in his place?" Blis said. "In the first place he speaks English intelligibly. That is a feat in itself, as you should be first to admit. Then consider what he has accomplished in the last twenty-four hours. He has got possession of Dot, in spite

61

of her being your elephant. He has gently forced Lem to ask you to take a back seat. He has discovered a wealthy patron in Gil Combs—wealthy by Haru's standards at any rate—and has secured an invitation to Florida and, probably, an employer for life. I think those are noteworthy accomplishments for a person you want to call subhuman. They verge on the superhuman to me, but I told Asa that perhaps we had better call him human until we had more evidence."

That was Blis all over, as balanced as a canary on a swing.

"Asa cheered right up," Blis went on. "He said in that case he could handle him. I promised you'd be there at 3 p.m. sharp, and said I'd follow with Haru, but he'd better keep you out of sight or Haru'd smell a trick."

"Haru won't go with you either, unless Gil goes," I said.

"Stop trying to run the universe and agree to something. Will you present yourself at Little Yellowstone at three?"

I agreed, though I knew it was just wasting an afternoon. Nobody could change Haru's mind about Dot, that was certain. But I was curious to know how Asa would try.

Stringy took me aside after lunch and asked if I minded being bat boy instead of short-stop. He said he'd found a boy who'd been playing short since he was six and knew the game. I told Stringy that suited me fine. I had enough on my mind with Dot and Haru and Gil and

Taddie and being junior counselor in general without spending my time on a ballfield. So, after rest hour, I got permission and paddled over to Little Yellowstone in a good hot sun.

CHAPTER VII

Maybe Mrs. Lirrup could change her mind to suit herself, but it wasn't so easy for me. Never yet had I crossed over to Little Yellowstone without something awful happening. So this time I tried to be as careful as a junior counselor ought to be.

I circled around through the trees to the back door. It was open and nobody in the kitchen. As I tiptoed across the floor, Asa's bird clock started to strike and scared me cold. Only the cuckoo and wren and one other bird were ducking out of their little doors and singing, so I made out it was three o'clock. I tiptoed into the hall. Suddenly I heard a voice whisper *skulks*. I guess I jumped three feet.

It was Mrs. Lirrup sitting at a little table and writing in a notebook. She's very forceful and repeats with her lips what she writes and that's why I heard *skulks*.

"Excuse me," I said. "I didn't see you."

"I've seen you, however." Mrs. Lirrup propped her chin on her hand and stared at me like she was taking measurements.

"Yes, ma'am. The time I came to get my elephant."

"Of course," and she wrote down *trespasses* forcefully. Then she studied me again and said, "I see you will be helpful. Now—you may answer this question frankly, without fear of punishment, however just. What had you in mind to steal?"

"Me? I wasn't going to steal anything, ma'am."

"Better than I hoped," she said to herself and wrote down, *Shuffles feet while equivocating*. She looked at me again. "I esteem frankness and I repeat, you have nothing to fear. What was it you came in so stealthily in order to appropriate, or in plainer language to rob me of?"

"I wasn't . . . I mean, I didn't, ma'am."

She wrote *Scratches left ear in confusion as dissimulation fails*. Then she said, "Was it the clock that struck your fancy?"

"I wouldn't take it for a gift," I said.

"Good, now we're getting somewhere. What is it you *would* like to take? Please feel perfectly free to confide."

"Is Asa home?" I asked. *He'd* tell her I wasn't a thief.

She didn't bother to answer but wrote *weak evasiveness when cornered*. "I too can change the subject," she said. "Perhaps you would rather answer this: in your boyish code, which crime gives you the greatest pleasure: housebreaking, thievery, or prevarication?"

"Is that you, Keetsie?" Asa Lirrup called from the cellar. "Come on down."

"You see, he was expecting me," I said.

Shows intense relief at unforeseen intervention went down in the notebook as Asa bounded up the stairs. "I see them coming," he said.

"My new project, Asa, is going to be distinctly valuable," Mrs. Lirrup said. "This boy has unwittingly divulged . . ."

"One moment, Mother," Asa said. "Come, Keetsie, Blis and Haru are landing. Follow me, please."

I needed no coaxing to leave Mrs. Lirrup. I didn't get her. That exposing business was too deep for me. It looked like she was exposing herself and it made me sore, but I didn't like to tell Asa for fear he'd think I was dumb. "You going to duck Haru in Young Faithful?" I asked.

"Do you make friends that way, Keetsie?" Asa smiled.

"You can't make friends with him. He's as slippery as they come. There's nothing about him you can take hold of."

"Are you sure you know Haru?" Asa asked quietly.

"How can you make friends with someone who changes sides all the time?"

"I think of Haru as being exceptionally loyal."

"You ought to see him. A weathervane isn't in it. First he calls me Worthy Master, and then it's Gil, and I don't exist."

Asa thought a moment. "Let's put it this way. Have

you ever been fond of anything, deeply, passionately fond?"

"Sure, I'm fond of Dot."

"And you have known her less than a week. Yet Haru has been devoted to her all his life."

"But now she's *mine!*" I said. It was funny nobody ever thought of that.

"She's yours," Asa said patiently. "In a way of speaking. But in slave days, if someone had bought you away from your mother, she'd still love you as hers, wouldn't she? The exchange of money would mean nothing to her, because she'd go on loving you. And so with Haru. He's bound to have his child back whatever happens. And because he's a very simple soul with instincts rather than thoughts, he can't tell you all this, but has to try to work it out for himself."

We heard footsteps upstairs and Asa said, "I'll hide you until we straighten this little misunderstanding out. By the way, I'll want you to paddle Haru back, as Blis is staying to supper—for Mother's convenience."

"Haru'd rather drown than get in the same canoe with me," I began, but Asa put his finger on his lips and led me to one of those hollow stumps he had made for bird-watching, with knotholes to see through. Haru followed Blis down and he was dark and handsome in a new turban.

"Asa," Blis said, "shake hands with Haru Panda, Dot's friend and protector, and a newcomer to our country."

67

Haru bowed and said, "Unworthy to intrude."

"I might add, he is elaborately humble," Blis said.

"The Worthless One," Haru murmured.

"I am glad to meet Your Worthlessness," Asa said. "It refreshes me to find someone with a head that remains unswollen. I have long wanted to talk with someone from your great India, Haru Panda. And you can bring me wisdom from the banks of Mother Ganges. This is a privilege, sir."

Well, they went on like that, but coming downgrade all the time, until they got too interested to be polite. Asa induced Haru to give us Dot's history. She had been a grown elephant, of course, when Haru was born. His father was an elephant keeper and when Haru was small, his father set a ladder against Dot and Haru climbed to her back. She would sway him to sleep like a hammock and pick fruit to hand him with her trunk.

Once when she was going down to bathe in the Ganges, he slipped off her back and fell on a slope of ground and rolled right under her. She did not even set down her foot lest she crush the child. Her soft warm trunk found his arm and pulled him out from under her. Then she gently slid her trunk beneath him, clasped him and raised him onto her head so that he could climb back to his seat.

"You were four or five then?" Asa asked.

Haru nodded, but he wasn't giving himself away.

"And you're about twenty now?"

Haru held out his brown hands and stared at his long

68

fingers. "Twenty, yes," he said, but you could see he didn't mean it. He was like Dot. You couldn't tell her age any more than the moon's.

Haru then gave Asa and Blis a long tale of the war and his master having to sell Dot, and he was thrown in. They were taken on a ship. Haru didn't like the ship, still less our country, and least of all the circus. He was outraged at seeing his Queen of All Created Elephants employed to amuse foreigners, and such loud ones! The bands hurt his ears and the peanut shells his feet. He was thankful each day the circus got poorer and more ragged, and he rejoiced when it folded up at Hoggset. He had not fore-seen the auction and he was desolated at being separated from Dot, his lifelong friend. Haru got excited and dramatic telling how he would have liked to strangle Sheriff Wickendorf for jailing him over a little parsley, when it was so necessary for him to go with Dot. The way Haru got his hands around Wickendorf's leathery neck—I mean as he was talking—was a caution. I almost thought Wickendorf was going to choke.

"You act as well as you talk," Asa said to Haru when he'd finished the show. "You have a most expressive voice, as fresh and delightful as running water. Will you make me a present of it?"

You should have seen Haru's face! It almost expressed something. I guess it was the first time anyone had ever asked him to give him his voice.

"I fail to understand, pestilence of stupidity that I am! What should I do without my voice, most learned one?"

"You'd still have it." Asa smiled. "I have a way of taking it that permits you to keep it."

Even I was a little bothered to understand that, but Blis smiled and nodded just as if Asa was talking sense. "Asa will keep it in a box, Haru, and Dot can listen to you speak even when you are a thousand miles away."

The wonders of this nonsense were making Haru's black eyes glisten. "My intelligence is very young, O fount of wisdom," he said to Asa. "It begs for pity on its knees. Kindly put what you have spoken more simply for the creature."

"Better still, I'll show you," Asa said. He lifted a cover from a machine, and I saw that he knew what he was talking about after all. "You may be incomparably worthless, Haru Panda," Asa went on. "But you have an agile imagination. I ask you to imagine your noble elephant standing there." He pointed to a spot in front of the recorder.

"It is done. She is there," Haru murmured.

"Now greet her lovingly, as if you had not seen her today."

Haru bowed in the direction of Dot and said something in his cooey way that sounded like a nest of love-birds waking up.

Asa listened until Haru finished. "Would it trouble you to tell us in our own unimportant language what you have said?"

Haru complied gladly. "O Queen of All Created Elephants, Gem of the Ganges, and Morning of Thy Worthless One's life, thy harebrained master salutes thee."

"Excellent!" Asa exclaimed. "I wish I were worth the honor of being an elephant, so that I might suitably be addressed in such terms. Now, will you explain to your beloved that your voice will remain in her ear no matter how far away you have to travel?"

"It shall be explained," Haru said. This time he made a longer speech and it sounded persuasive.

Again Asa asked Haru to interpret his words. My servant took a long breath and said, "Listen deeply, first and last Elephant of my Heart. My voice hath decided to live with thee, lest thou be lonely in my absence. It will tremble in thy hearing when I am as far as the Himalayas are from the sea. These pale barbarians, little mouse, have eaten knowledge. They do wondrous things. They kindle their lamps from waterfalls. They are drawn through the streets by invisible horses. They follow Mahomet across the sky in loud flocks. They bewitch boxes so that spirits come before them to tell them what may be bought on the morrow and for how much. They have such plenty to eat that their bellies are like well-tuned drums. And now, sweet mite, they arrange for my voice to comfort thee when I am not there, so that thou shalt obey as if I were behind it, as usual."

"What if Dot does not obey?" Blis asked.

"Unworthy as I am, she takes pity on my poor wishes and does obey them."

"Again thy profound imagination," Asa said. "In pretense, she is not obeying. She is stubborn. You command her to walk with you, and she refuses. What then?"

71

Haru jumped into the part. He frowned and drew himself up, almost to Blis's chin, and growled out, "Oh, thou ungrateful insect, come! *Come*, I say, thou lump of lizard meat. Follow me! This little foot, and then that little foot. It is well. I shall reward thee for this with a bun dripping with sugar." Haru turned proudly to Asa and said, "She obeys."

"But wait, again she stops!" Asa said coldly.

"It is true! She has deceived me!" Haru agreed, and now his voice sank to a hoarse whisper. "Monster of sloth! Hast thou grown fast to the ground? Wilt thou not come? Or must I call the hungry one?" Haru waited with every part of his face tense, but Dot gave no sound of hearing. So Haru crouched low and called softly, "Here, tiger, tiger, tiger! Lick thy chops. Thy dinner waits for thee. It cools. Come quickly and eat. Come devour this stubborn beast!" Suddenly Haru sprang to his feet with a screech! "Quick! Quick! my love! The striped one is behind. He gathers his strength to spring. Save me! Save thyself! *Run!*" Once more his voice changed to a purr. "Good, my sweetheart, we are saved! Thou art swift! He shall not catch us now. . . . No, no, not *so* fast, my swallow, or I shall slide under thy feet. There, that is better. Stay!"

I almost forgot I was hiding in the stump and nearly applauded for Haru beat any actor I ever saw. I could smell the tiger. It sure was a narrow escape!

Blis grinned and clapped Haru on the shoulder. "Boy, you had me frightened. Dot was just one jump ahead there for a minute. You should put that act in television, and clean up." Blis turned to Asa. "Do you think an invisible elephant would televise well?"

Asa was occupied in getting ready to play Haru's voice back to him, and when that happened, Haru's face was something to see. His voice came back clear and cooey and then very angry. When Haru shouted at Dot for not moving, it sent shivers up and down my back, and when the tiger charged it was even worse. I didn't wonder Dot obeyed—I mean on the record.

Haru was entranced by his performance. "That my Pearl of the Punjabi must hear!" he said. "I must see her when I stand to one side and my voice comes from the other. May I carry my voice to her, O worker of wonders?"

"For a price," Asa said.

"Alas, I have no money," Haru said sadly.

"A price you can pay," Asa said. "Answer me this, Most Worthless of all. Why do you wish to be called worthless when you are smart as a trap?"

Haru looked startled but he said, "In my country, it is shameless not to be humble."

"How humble are you?"

"Demand, and see."

"I'll take you on that," Asa said. "My friend Blis wishes to stay for supper. My friend Keets has been visiting here and wishes to go home. Will you humble yourself to the point of allowing Keets to paddle you home?"

I was watching Haru's face for a sign of humility.

"Demand of me something else, O Friend of Wisdom and Patience," he said. "But not that. That one, he is a thief. He tries to steal the love of my Jewel of the Jungle. Seek of me anything else."

Well, that started a bargaining match I never expected to see—for me. Haru wanted his voice. Asa wanted him to call me Worthy Master, instead of Gil, and to recognize my elephant rights.

It was some struggle, and Asa was very patient. He kept reminding Haru that it was thanks to me that he had access to Dot at all. Finally, while they still argued, Blis played Haru's voice back to him again and that did the trick.

A sound upstairs interrupted. "Has Mother suddenly decided to move all the furniture around again?" Asa asked.

"I'm afraid it's thunder," Blis said.

"Take Haru to the dock and I'll bring Keets," Asa said to Blis, and to Haru, "You'll have your voice in about three weeks."

I was as stiff as a clothespin standing still all that time, but I sure was thankful to Asa. He said not to thank him yet, for Haru had only taken the hook and we still had to land him. I told him the hook was in deep and it was probably the first time anyone had bit on his own voice. I asked Asa how he'd thought of it.

"The minute Blis told me that Haru was human, I knew I had him," Asa said confidently. "To sit back and hear

74

yourself order a dumb animal around is something mighty few people can withstand."

"Well, I'll try not to hog Dot," I said.

"Thanks, Keetsie," Asa said. "That's what I wanted to hear. And there ought to be enough of her to go round."

CHAPTER VIII

Mrs. Lirrup called Asa upstairs to help close the windows, so by the time we reached Blis and Haru at the dock, the sky was a deep violetish color over towards camp.

"Can you make it all right?" Asa asked.

"Sure," I said. I knew Asa wanted to stay by his mother who didn't like thunderstorms, because she couldn't order them around, I guess.

Blis held the canoe for Haru to step in. He was pretty jaunty about it and stepped on the side, as if it was a warship or something. Blis went red in the face holding it. I could tell that Haru hadn't been in canoes much, for any hen would've known better. I saw Blis's lips moving, but he held in what he was going to say, because we all wanted to keep Haru sweet, now we'd gotten him there.

I stepped in and Blis thanked me for saving him the trip, and I thanked him and Asa, for they knew what,

76

and Asa thanked Haru and invited him and Dot to drop in at any time. Haru soaked it all up as quiet as a shadow and I pushed off. But the storm hadn't been idle. It seemed to have come up a lot and got darker. The sky would have made ink look kind of pale and sickly.

Haru's back was towards it, which was lucky, as Blis told me he had the artistic temperament and got nervous without notice. He held onto the gunwales with long graceful fingers and watched my paddle shoving her along so we made a wake. He wasn't a bad-looking Indian close up. His cheeks weren't chubby but longish and a nice walnut brown. His lips were thin and red and curved like a bow and he had a straight handsome nose. His eyes were very dark and didn't give him away at all. I guess they made his schoolteachers pretty mad, for they couldn't get a thing on him from the way he looked. I couldn't tell a single opinion he had of me now.

It was a good time to talk. If I hadn't had to push the canoe so fast we could have got together on something. But now I couldn't think of a subject. I didn't know how Dot would go down, or Gil, or Florida, or even the sheriff. Haru hated him like quick poison and we could agree on that. Also I wanted to compliment him on his acting in the Lirrup cellar, but then I'd have given Asa away, and he mightn't have liked being spied on. But finally I thought of something he couldn't object to and said, "Isn't that turban hot?"

Thunder drowned out what he said, though I knew he said it, for his teeth flashed white against the storm. He turned around to look at the cloud, very free and easy in his movements, as if he had been sitting on Dot, and the canoe gave a bad lurch.

"Watch out, unless you want to swim!" I shouted, for he scared me.

"I only swim on Dot," he said.

"You mean you can't swim?" That worried me even more.

"Yes."

"Yes you can't? Or yes you can?"

"That is what I say. I sink. I go down . . . down . . . down." He took his hands from the gunwale to show me how gracefully he eddied to the bottom. He was an artist all right.

That was nice! The wind clouds were boiling overhead and we weren't much past the middle of the lake, and the best he could think of was to illustrate how he sank in water.

"You've no right to be in a canoe, if you can't swim," I said. "You heard Mr. Pickerel give the rules."

Lightning sizzled around like a showerbath of fire, and Haru nearly upset the canoe by craning around again.

"*Sit still!*" I yelled and dug my paddle down deep to steady her.

"The monsoon approaches!" Haru said. "Hurry, if Worthy Master pleases!"

"What do you think I'm doing?" I gasped out.

"My Necklace of Beauty will wish me beside her."

"In India . . . don't you have thunderstorms?"

78

"Yes, yes, whole villages are washed away."

"Then Dot won't mind a little Maine gust." Little, was good.

Suddenly the sky opened like a furnace door and showed up the insides of the universe white hot.

"It comes!" Haru cried. "Faster, please! Push it faster!"

I bit my lips to keep from expressing myself.

"The loud boat went better. It could hurry," Haru said.

That's just too bad, I thought, but didn't say it. We were nearly there now, and I didn't want to spoil it all by any hasty remarks.

All at once a new sound came from the shore. It was Dot. She let out a sort of mellow bellow, very plaintive.

That was too much for Haru. "She calls! Make haste! She calls for me! Cannot Worthy Master exert himself?" I guess he was more sensitive than I thought for he whirled around and knelt quickly on the seat and made a trumpet of his hands to call back to her. I dug into the water with all I had, but it was not enough. Half way through his call, Haru lost balance, grabbed at the side, missed, and over we went in a slow-motion slide. At the same time the tempest descended in a smother of wind, lightning, thunder, and stinging cold rain.

We were so near shore that when I struck bottom and stood up the water came only to my shoulders. But that meant up to Haru's chin, and the waves slopped over that. I saw him thrashing his arms and try to yell and then he'd get a mouthful of water and choke.

"Stand up . . . *stand still!*" I yelled to him.

He was too scared to listen. He reached out to grab me, but I was holding the canoe and the wind pulled me a few steps away. "I drown . . . I drown!" he gurgled and then swallowed more of the lake.

"Shut your mouth and stand *still!*" I shouted.

"Help! Help! I drown!" he gurgled again and thrashed around. The rain pelted so hard it half blinded me. It was so thick you couldn't tell where the lake ended and the air began. Haru reached for me again, and again the wind dragged me. "Don't . . . don't," he cried, choking, and then went under.

I guessed I'd better let the canoe go and push Haru ashore, or he'd drown standing up. So I shoved the canoe

80

towards shore and came up behind Haru. "Stand up . . . Let your feet down!" I bellowed in his ear, for the water was only up to his waist here. But he kept thrashing and grabbing at me, and I knew I mustn't let him tangle with me or we both might drown.

"Down!" I shouted. "Let 'em down!" and I bent over and pushed his feet to the bottom so he could feel it. He gurgled but he got it. He felt bottom and stood up, gulping, choking, and still trying to grab me. The minute I saw he could stand, I raced over to the canoe and hauled it up on shore. When I got back to Haru he was on his hands and knees crawling out.

He raised himself and glared at me and said, "I escape. You do not drown me. I escape."

What with the thunder and swash of rain, I didn't think I heard him right. "What?" I shouted.

"I escape. See? You try drown Haru, but I escape. See?" His dark eyes snapped in vindictive excitement.

"You crazy loon! I saved your worthless life, if you come down to it," I shouted.

"I drown . . . you watch. I go to you. You leave Haru. You laugh to see Haru drown. But I escape."

"You must have hit your head!" I said.

"I tell Worthy Master Gil. I tell everybody you want Haru drown. Then you have Dot. See?"

I was starting to shiver and so was he. "Go dry off and you'll feel better." I thought he was really scared nutty.

"I tell . . ." he began.

"Here's Mr. Pickerel. Tell him!" I shouted, for I saw

81

him coming towards us in yellow oilskins with a hood.

"I escape! I escape!" Haru cried to Mr. Pickerel. "He try drown me, but I escape."

"You escaped, all right—from a lunatic asylum!" Mr. Pickerel told him. "We saw you upset the canoe and refuse to wade ashore." Then he turned to me. "Keets, you handled that situation like a man. Now go and get dry things on. I'll attend to this id . . ."

A thunderbolt blotted out Mr. Pickerel's further remarks. Then Dot trumpeted again and Haru called back something in Indian and ran to his pet.

Mr. Pickerel said, "Don't let him get your goat, Keets. A dozen of us in the bungalow saw the whole thing. Lem is grateful to you. Now beat it."

I loped up the trail to my tent. I was set up by what Mr. Pickerel had said, because he's not one to hand out free praise. But I felt sort of saddish, too, for Haru had it in for me worse than ever. He couldn't understand that the wind and canoe had pulled me away, and he didn't know I daren't let him grab me. He really believed I wanted him to drown and we were back where we started, only worse. For now all Asa's work had been for nothing.

Things were quieter in my tent than I expected. I guess it was the lightning. Even Forman wasn't going to act sour when any minute he might be ripped to pieces, though he did say, "Don't you know enough to come in out of the rain?"

"I'm glad somebody dug the rain trench," I said. "Who did it?"

"I did," Taddie spoke up. "But Dempsy helped."

Sprigg laughed. "Taddie *showed* Dempsy where to dig. He's a born junior counselor."

"Where's Rugg?"

"Nature Boy Rugg is out observing the storm," Forman said. "That makes two of a kind."

Well, I didn't mind their cracks and all I said was, "The worst I could wish you, Forman, is that you'd be made junior counselor." The job was a man trap.

Faint and far away through the downpour I heard Silas's bugle, first call for supper.

"How do we get there?" Taddie asked.

"That's easy," Dempsy said. "We go with the current. Coming back we have to fight it."

It ended up with Dempsy carrying Taddie. Silas must have known it was going to turn cold, for we had pork chops and hot chocolate and hot brown betty with hard sauce for dessert. Downy happened to say that the pork chops would melt in your mouth, and Taddie filled his mouth with one and waited to see, which held up his table some.

After supper we had a dandy fire in the bungalow. Lem told us about the Camp Chesunquoik point system. You got points for improvement in swimming and diving and canoeing and making a fire in the rain and so forth. The first pay-off came in mid-season and was a choice of

83

anything you wanted from the Campers Catalogue, up to a certain price.

"But you didn't come here to pick up points," Lem cautioned. "You came to have fun and be a good guy without knowing you are, if you get me. Mr. Wieldy says that you can get the lowdown on your abilities by doing what you want to do here and doing it with all your heart, and there's something in it."

I sure hoped that wasn't true or I'd have a terrible time in life, the way I was going.

Then Lem and Mr. Pickerel organized a show and everybody got into it. Only we nearly laughed ourselves sick, especially when our tent had to put on an act showing how we got Taddie down to breakfast on time. The evening ended with Silas revealing how he saved his life when he was being chased by a lion in Abyssinia. He kept throwing it sticky cinnamon buns and the lion couldn't resist the temptation to catch them. Silas had brought in a big tray of hot cinnamon buns and threw one to each boy to demonstrate, and Lem handed around mugs of gingerale as a chaser. It was the best time we'd had yet and Taddie said he hoped it would rain every night.

CHAPTER IX

I woke up dreaming I was sliding downhill on an avalanche, but it was just Sprigg and Forman dumping my cot. Then we dumped Dempsy and Taddie and Rugg who happened to be present. Everybody felt so good on account of the sun and nippy air that the fights were laughing fights. Even Taddie dressed so fast you could tell what he was doing.

I raced breakfast down because I wanted to see whether Haru was going to live up to his word to Asa and Blis, or blame me for choking on lake water. I slowed down near the stockade and the sight I saw nearly put out my eyes. Dot was standing in the sun and wearing her howdah, and its crimson and gold blazed like a campfire. Dot looked haughtier than I'd ever seen her. I heard a song being hummed from somewhere. Then I spotted Haru lying in the shadow under Dot's belly where he was finishing the fastening of the howdah belts.

At last he crawled out and stood up and cocked his head, the way Blis does at a work of art, and said, "There, my tiny one, my little Lotus Flower, now thou art royal again!" He flicked a dab of mud from Dot's hind leg with his long middle finger. "Now show thy majesty to that jackal who tried to drown me, encased in pants as I was. He will fear to lift his hand against thy servant."

So that was his tune, trying to poison my character to Dot! Murdo was right: Haru was a two-timer. I didn't know what to do. Dot caught my scent and spoke to me and Haru jumped around and saw me.

"Good morning, Haru," I said, as if I wasn't a jackal. "How's everything?"

No lamb ever put on such a look of meekness as he arranged on his traitor face. "Worthy Master has come in time to direct his servants."

Well, I guess Mr. Pickerel must have given him a whale of a talking to. "How did you ever get it up there?" I asked, for the howdah made Dot look taller than ever.

"Kneel, my Lotus Leaf," Haru said. "Worthy Master despises our intelligence."

Dot's great crinkly knees bent slowly and she lowered her four tons to the ground. Haru had made it plain who despised whose intelligence, and I had to hand it to him for letting me know in a roundabout way. But not so roundabout that I'd miss it, for I heard him mutter that even the young of the baboon could figure that out.

"Will Worthy Master choose to be first to ride?" Haru asked. That made me feel better. Let him think I was a jackal, just so he lived up to his agreement with Asa and Blis.

"We can go see the baseball practice," I suggested.

"We are a carpet for Worthy Master to walk on," Haru said. Mr. Pickerel had sure set him straight on the drowning. Even on the day I'd saved Dot from the auction Haru hadn't sounded as oily as this. I didn't exactly want him to feel like a carpet, but it was a relief after having him so uppity.

Haru indicated how to get up, by holding his two hands like a stirrup for me to put my foot in. Then we hoisted together, and I clutched the rim of the howdah and climbed in. Dot sat as patient as a hypnotized snail. Then at Haru's command she lifted up as easy as a sunrise. I wondered how many times she could do push-ups. We had forgotten one thing—the tree branches at the entrance. I had to wait until Haru found a hatchet. Then I leaned out of the howdah and chopped our way clear. It took an hour to widen the passage for the howdah.

The woods smelled fine after the rain. Dot plucked a twig now and then as we sashayed up the trail to the road and the ballfield. The howdah swayed and Dot marched as if she heard stately music. When we came out into the sunlight on the ballfield, I never felt showier, like a bee in a tulip. I wished my class at school could see me. I guess nothing makes you prouder than owning an elephant and an Indian servant walking along down below, that is, when all your troubles are over.

Mr. Pickerel's organization had done a swell job on

the ballfield. He'd got the farmer to mow it and roll it, and the boys had limed the lines and tied the bags down. It looked like the pictures of the Braves', only without the stadium, and you kind of expected to hear the stand boys selling pop and programs.

I directed Haru to lead Dot around back of home plate to where the camp was watching the practice. She walked like an empress with her crown on, very royal and haughty, and Blis was quick to see which way the wind was blowing. What with me riding in state and Haru looking mouse meek, he gathered that all was jake and sang out, "Rajah Keets in person!"

Murdo caught on just as fast and called out, "Our Mascot, fellows! Let's give a Chesunquoik Airsplitter for Dot. One—*two!*"

By that time the practice was pretty well broken up and the team came crowding in. Our yell, which Downy made up, is an air-splitter all right and it ended with "Dot . . . *Dot* . . . DOT . . . *DOT!*" Haru prompted Dot and she curled her trunk back and trumpeted. The whole camp cheered and I felt like that Roman Emperor in History V back from the wars.

One boy hadn't come in, though—Gil Combs. He was standing on the mound with his arms akimbo and his face was poached-egg white. He was sore as a spiked foot. He couldn't figure out what had happened, but it was plain he had lost Haru and Dot, and Florida might as well be Greenland for all the good it did him. He was growing tired of posing out there with nobody paying attention and called out, "What is this, a ball game or a zoo?"

"You're jealous!" Sprigg shouted back and the others laughed.

"What the heck of?" Gil called, but no one needed to answer. Even Forman's face showed he took it all back—about his doubts of my owning Dot, that is. That made me feel so good that I had to divide with someone. I saw Taddie trying to look up Dot's trunk. He wanted to see what the inside led to. So I told him to stand by and requested Dot to hand him up. Dot delivered Taddie aloft, shrieking with joy, and I helped him climb into the howdah.

"All right, fellows, let's go," Stringy said. So they went back to their positions, and Mr. Pickerel asked me to park Dot behind the bats.

"That is as Worthy Master wishes," Haru said to Mr. Pickerel. Haru sure had swung over to me. Mr. Pickerel shot an impulsive glance at him but swallowed his impudence for the common good.

Haru led Dot well beyond the foul line and Dempsy stood by Dot in case she needed help. Dempsy would have stopped growing if he couldn't help somebody. It was a good trait, even if four times out of five he was a nuisance. The fifth time more than made up for it.

By now Gil had condescended to unlock his arms and work. He was on fire on account of seeing his plans smashed up. I couldn't thank Asa enough for taking the trouble with Haru's voice. Gil burned his pitches in to Stringy and nobody could get a piece of the ball.

"Good going, boy!" Stringy yelled after three vicious pitches had retired Murdo. "Keep lining 'em in like that and Hoggset'll never see a hit." Stringy didn't know how much Dot and I were helping. I wondered how I could make Gil equally mad the day of the game. He could beat the Braves if he lost his temper bad enough.

Presently Sprigg nipped the ball for a foul and it rolled to Dot's foot. Dempsy grabbed it up and then had a bright idea. He held it out to Dot and said, "Throw it in, babe." Haru spoke to Dot and she took it off Dempsy's palm, like a peanut, but instead of hoisting it into her mouth she swung her trunk and let go and the ball rolled straight to Gil. The fellows had been watching and Murdo shouted, "Kick Gil off the mound, Stringy. You've got a pitcher now!"

"Try her at bat!" Forman suggested.

"Boy, could she go round those bases!" Sprigg said.

"Train her to slide, Mr. Pickerel," Dempsy called.

"Her hide could stand it," Murdo said, and they laughed again.

Gil had been heating up once more and now he threw down his glove. "The heck with it!" he said. "I'm going for a swim."

"Get back there," Stringy said.

"This is no practice," Gil said and walked on. He was

90

so serious that any fun not in the line of duty burned him up.

Well, they pacified him at last by giving in about Dot. Gil said he wouldn't play unless they kicked the lousy elephant and her stinking keeper off the field, and he made sure Haru heard. It surprised me that a nice guy like Gil could use such words about his late friends. Haru didn't turn a hair. He looked like one of those gravestones the rain has washed the words off of. Naturally I wasn't mad at the way things were going and I asked Dempsy up in the howdah too.

Mr. Pickerel apologized to Dot and me for asking us to leave the ballfield, but he said he knew I'd do anything to help the team. I'd seen enough anyway to feel hopeful about beating Hoggset. Stringy was an ace catcher, with a swell peg to second, and Gil would surprise Snag Wickendorf if we could only keep him sore.

The camp gave Dot another Air-Splitter as we left the field, and Haru bowed. I invited Taddie and Dempsy to stay aloft, and it was a pleasure to see how new elephant riding was to them. Dot was plenty satisfied and purred like one of those concrete-mixers. Taddie kept asking when the tiger was going to spring at us. It seems that Downy had connected elephants in Taddie's mind with tiger-hunts.

I wanted Silas to see the howdah, so we went by his tent, and Haru went in to pick up a cooler turban. Silas came out and stood stock still in front of the howdah. "You sure are fixed up now, Mr. Keets," he said. "All gold and glory and going places for certain! I pays my respects."

Taddie called down for Silas to come up, too. Silas favored Taddie because he was always last through at meals. It showed that he appreciated them, Silas said. Taddie kept shrieking for Silas to climb up.

"Now, Mr. Taddie, you're mixed in the head! Which *is* the elaphunt, me or her?"

Taddie laughed so hard that he lost his balance and toppled out of the howdah onto Dot's neck. Dot didn't even act surprised. She curled up her trunk and steadied Taddie until Dempsy and I could haul him back. I noticed Haru standing in the tent entrance with his arms twined up, looking mad. I guess he didn't hold to children using Dot as a gymnasium and you couldn't blame him.

When we neared Mr. Wieldy's tent, he looked out to see why the earth was shaking. His mumps had gone down a lot. Mr. Wieldy was a fine-looking young man when he didn't bulge. He said to me, "I'd salaam, if my anatomy permitted. You look imperial this morning." He noticed Haru's glumness and said to him, "Thanks, Mr. Panda, for completing the uniqueness of Camp Chesunquoik, the Camp with a Difference. We now have a waiting-list of boys largely because of Dot and her wise and hand-some trainer. We appreciate your care of these boys and will not forget it at the end of the summer."

Mr. Wieldy knew how to soften a fellow up and Haru turned several shades less glum. Lem came along and asked Haru if Dot would haul a backlog for the Council

Fire. So we left and I felt on top of the world, including Dot.

After ball practice we all had a swim and Dot, too, after Haru took off the howdah. She was as playful as a kitten. Blis said that if everybody knew what a nice pet an elephant made, there'd be one in every home, unless it was an apartment, that is.

Dot made up a water game. She pretended she was being attacked by hyenas and kept us off by blowing water at us, and a fire hose couldn't have done it better. Only Taddie she allowed on her back. The rest of us hyenas couldn't get within three trunk-lengths of her.

Taddie almost had hysterics the way Dot'd churn around in the water and squirt floods at us. Once he slipped off but Dot reached around and lifted him up before we could close in. Haru watched from the shore. Water didn't appeal to him much unless it was in the Ganges, especially after the thunderstorm.

Nobody could have more fun than we did and nobody cared who owned Dot any more. I felt smoothed out and happy, except for one thing—Gil. He sulked off by himself a lot. Murdo kidded Stringy about it, but Stringy stood up for Gil, for it was serious having your star pitcher feeling too cranky. What worried me was it gave Gil time to think, and there's nothing more dangerous than that. I didn't like it, though, as I say, I was happy in most other directions.

CHAPTER X

The days leading up to the game slid by so fast you couldn't tell them apart. Blis got Downy and Quizzy and some of the new boys to help him make BEAT HOGG-SET banners and tied them across the trails and in the dining-tent where you couldn't help seeing them. He painted a special banner to fasten on front of the howdah. If we didn't beat Hoggset, you couldn't lay it to Blis and his crew.

Nor to Stringy, either. Nine rat terriers, with plenty of rats, wouldn't have worked harder than the Chesunquoik Braves. It wasn't safe on the field. Not only was the first nine playing the second, but subs were practicing for all the positions, and several pitchers and catchers kept warming up in case Gil broke his arm. Taddie got conked, and Silas just escaped being brained by a pitcher whose curve beat the Horseshoe Bend.

Being bat boy was trickier than I supposed. The bats

were probably different, like robins. But it'd take a detective to pick out anybody's particular robin, and the same with bats. I picked up some new expressions when I handed out the wrong bat. They ought to have hired a mind-reader. Finally I got a way of telling the bats apart. I stuck a snitch of spruce gum on the letter that stood for the owner's name—like on the S in Spalding for Stringy, and it paid off.

"You've got a good eye," Stringy told me.

"I can miss," I said. I thought the gum would rub off.

"If you had that eye at the plate, I could use you as pinchhitter."

"I don't see moving objects so well," I said.

It didn't work, after all. The fellows couldn't be content to hold their bat, they had to fondle it and got messed up. They told me to lay off chewing gum if I couldn't help smearing it over their bats. They weren't intelligent enough to know I had a purpose.

The day before the game Blis brought out a BEAT HOGGSET edition of the Chesunquoik Buzz, and it was a hummer. For a sub-title he put SOUTHPAW SPECIAL to compliment Gil. He drew each member of the team in some typical position—Catcher Stringy squatting, and first base Forman reaching for a high one, and Gil winding up, and so forth. Mr. Pickerel said it was a collector's item.

Asa had run Murdo down to Hoggset so he could check up on Snag Wickendorf's team and Blis got Murdo to write up his impressions. It was the slickest piece I've

95

seen this side of the Boston *Globe*. Silas asked me what language it was written in. He didn't know that firemen were relief pitchers, or a jug handle was a wide-breaking curve ball. He thought sneakers were shoes instead of deceptive fast balls. When Murdo wrote, "Snag kept feeding his banjo hitter the dead mackerel," Silas said he didn't know they took time out for lunch. He sure was ignorant, so I translated the whole piece for him and Silas said, "Mr. Murdo is a lot more learned than I suspicioned."

Forman had also ridden to Hoggset with Lem and had talked to some of the natives while Lem was buying groceries. Forman let on he had heard there was a game coming up and wrote down a few of the boasts about what Snag's team was going to do to us city slickers. It made hot reading. Blis scattered the team members' comments on these boasts through the pages.

Blis did another smart thing. He interviewed Haru and wrote it up and let Haru sign it. He called it "Timely Tips for Elephant Sitters." Haru was so pleased at having a piece in the paper that he carried a copy wherever he went. I thought this sewed Haru up for certain, especially as Haru called me Worthy Master all the time now and Gil never mentioned Dot or Florida. I didn't notice that Gil had stopped sulking and should have taken the hint.

We had a Pep Rally the night before the game. It had come on to rain, so we held it in the bungalow, and the mosquitoes crowded in too. Murdo called them satellites to make fun of Quizzy who was always talking about such things. "You scientists are a crummy-headed bunch," he told Quizzy. "Why don't you make this planet worth living on instead of setting out for Mars? How do you know the mosquitoes up there aren't six feet long and sound like electric drills?"

"We don't *know*. That's why we're scientists: to find out," Quizzy came back. "I'd rather like to see a mosquito six feet long."

Lem rapped for order and asked Stringy to say a few words about the game. Then Gil Combs said a few more. And then the others. It sure was a beautiful victory after they'd got done with it, and Silas was mighty excited. He'd never been to a pep rally before, and believed everything he heard. When he could understand it, that is.

"Taking one on the meat . . . taking one on the meat . . . Now just exactly what does that mean, Mr. Keets?" So I told him it was a guy at bat hit by a pitched ball.

"It's funny they can't say what they mean, being eddicated the way they are. Now listen to Mr. Murdo talking about giving the old apple a ride. What's an apple care if it's riding or not?"

I no sooner explained that than Gil got up and said a few biting things about Snag's pitching. Silas was puzzled worse than ever. "He's says that fellow Snag's got nothing on the ball but the cover. What's he *want* on it anyways?"

It was hard explaining curves to Silas when I wanted to hear Gil. Mr. Pickerel closed the rally with a few words. He was pretty quiet, after the boys, and didn't even promise we'd win. He thanked everybody for giving all they had to the practices. Then he read a telegram from Mr. Wieldy. That's what he called it, though Mr. Wieldy was only four tents away. The telegram said, "My best wishes for Camp Chesunquoik's first game of the season. Have fun and a clean game. If two teams don't part with more respect for each other than when they started, they've lost the best part of the sport. Wieldy."

That was a funny thing to say and the fellows didn't like being calmed off like that.

"Hooey!" Forman said.

"Let's be perfect gentlemen!" Murdo said and everybody laughed.

"The mumps must be affecting his brain," Gil remarked.

"How many teams love each other like that?" Stringy demanded.

"I thought you had more sense," Blis said to these four. "Can't you admire anyone's playing but your own?"

"Sure, if it's better," Stringy said.

"That's what Mr. Wieldy's saying."

"Give it the bottle," Forman said.

"Let's close with Hymn 24," Murdo cracked, and they laughed.

"What do you play a game for?" Lem asked Murdo.

"To beat the stuffing out of the other fellows," Murdo said.

"How?" Lem asked quietly.

That stumped Murdo for a moment. "By beating them

to it. By having more on the ball. Is that what you mean?"

"In other words, by your skill," Lem said. "You match your ability against your opponent's ability to see whose ability wins. Isn't that it?"

"No!" shouted half a dozen voices. And one boy yelled, "It's you—not just your ability. It's the fight you put up."

"Lem's right, though," Blis said. "All that has to be expressed through your skill, doesn't it?"

Well, they were just about to admit there might be a glimmer of sense in Mr. Wieldy's telegram when Sprigg shouted, "Here comes the real champ!" It was Silas carrying a tray of Scotch wafers, as big around as a dinner plate, made of molasses and things, and as sticky and chewy and good, as possible.

Blis started to argue why a team gave a yell for the other team at the end of a game, win or lose, if it wasn't respect, but he made the mistake of biting into a wafer and lost his powers of speech. The other arguers couldn't talk much better.

I slipped out to find Haru and tell him who I'd like to ride with me to the game in the howdah. He wasn't in his tent, so he was probably in the stockade with Dot. He usually had a goodnight talk with Dot before he went to bed.

The rain had changed to fog, thick as cotton, and I had to let my feet pick the trail. It was spooky with drops of water plopping from the branches and no wind. Presently I heard a slush-slush ahead of me, and then a slop-slop,

99

and then a slump-slump. It raised the hair on my neck right up. It sounded like an animal, but any animal making clumsy noises like that, didn't know its business.

Suddenly a voice not far ahead of me said, "Where in mud are you?" It was Gil.

"This way, Worthy Master," said Haru soft as a feather.

I stopped short, for it isn't polite to interrupt. Gil barged into a bush, I guess, for I heard sticks breaking and some remarks.

"Now this way, Worthy Master," Haru said.

When he repeated Worthy Master, that did it. That opened my blind eyes and burned me up like a blow-torch. He had been putting it over on me all the time. Neither of them had changed.

Gil thrashed around and reached the stockade. "Now where in night are you?"

"Just here, noble friend."

"What if I bump into Dot?"

"I have told her."

"Keep talking."

"Now you're on my foot," Haru said sweetly.

It made me sick to hear them. It was so still I could hear their lowest whisper. They were making plans for the game. Gil was to ride to Hoggset in the howdah and he would invite Stringy, Forman, and Sprigg. If Lem or the jackal—that was my name now—raised so much as a yelp, Haru was to say that he couldn't take Dot.

100

This was a nice surprise, after nearly two weeks of thinking my troubles were over. And it was all a riddle to me. What had changed Haru back again to Gil? What could Gil give Haru that was better than his voice?

I was too sore and upset to stand still, so I hunted the way back to my tent and ran into Murdo coming out. "You're a swell junior counselor," he said with a grin. "Where've you been hacking around?"

Murdo made you feel good. He always pretended you were doing something you shouldn't. "Come back for a visit," I said.

"Too many ears," he said. "I looked for you before the rally, but no find. There's something going on I don't like, Keetsie. I'm on supper squad, you know, and Silas sent me to his tent for the glove he lifts kettles with. I heard Gil in there. He and Haru were snarling at each other."

"Snarling!" I couldn't believe it after the cooey stuff I'd just heard.

"Sure, snarling, like a couple of tigers when you poke them with a stick. Gil kept saying, 'Then it's all off . . . I won't take you . . . Forget it!' and Haru would say, 'But my voice! They keep my voice. I won't have my voice.' Then Gil said, 'I can give you a better voice. I can give you Dot's voice.' But that didn't faze Haru. So Gil said, "All right . . . Forget it, I say . . . Stay here in the sticks . . . Stay with the jackal if you love him so much . . . Stay and freeze, and see if I care . . .' A couple of loonies'd make more sense."

So I told Murdo that the trip Gil was calling off, was to Florida, and about Asa's making the record of Haru's voice.

"That takes a load off my mind," Murdo said with a grin. "Then they're nuts and not me."

"But they've made up," I said, and told Murdo about Gil's arrangements for the howdah passengers.

"We can fix that," Murdo said angrily. "Come, we'll go beat them up. I can punch sense into Gil and you can knock Haru silly."

"That's no good. Besides, Gil's got to pitch tomorrow."

"All the better," Murdo said. "I'll threaten to beat him up, unless he lays off Haru, pitching or no pitching."

"It's no good, I tell you," I said. "It would get Lem down on us."

"Gil wouldn't fight. He wants to pitch too much. He'd back down."

"I'm not at all sure."

"Let's see."

I had an awful time holding Murdo back, especially as I didn't want to, though I knew a fight wouldn't do any good and probably would make things worse. The only reason Murdo didn't bump Gil's head off was the fact that Murdo wanted to beat Hoggset so much.

"Doggone it!" he said finally. "Why didn't Asa make a record of Dot. Then we'd have Haru sewed up. Now we've got to think of something bigger than Florida to bribe him with."

"There's India," I suggested. But Murdo didn't see how we were going to work India in.

"The worst of it is, I've kind of half promised a ride in the howdah to Taddie and Quizzy."

"Lem will be just as sore as I am," Murdo predicted. "We'll see him first thing in the morning. He'll fix things up."

It made me feel good to hear Murdo say that, for it meant he saw Lem's good points now and Murdo had been pretty sour on Lem. It was too late to hunt Lem up now, so we turned in.

Next morning made the night seem like a bad dream. There wasn't a cloud, and the heat had been turned on to make good baseball. Lem was so busy after breakfast that Murdo and I had to wait to tell him about the howdah mess. We told Blis, of course, and he went with us.

Lem never shows when he's sore, at least not the way Pop does. Pop comes out boiling, but Lem draws in, and you have to read between his words. He listened to us, and you might suppose it was just another weather report. Instead of going up in the air he said, "That's an interesting development. I wonder what salary Gil is going to demand for running this camp."

Blis looked at me and winked. He knew Lem was foaming with rage, he took such pains not to show it.

"It would be simpler not to take Dot," Lem said. "That would settle the rides question."

"I'd rather Gil would ride than Dot not go," I said.

Lem looked sharply at me. "You would." I could tell he was pleased.

"Dot's our mascot," Blis said. "She's half the fun of going."

"Let me fix it," Murdo offered. "I can't beat up Gil before the game, but I can warn him about later."

Lem gazed at Murdo with his thick black hair, black eyebrows, and enthusiastic black eyes. "Still primitive Neanderthal," Lem said. "By rights we should keep you in a cave and feed you raw meat." He turned to Blis and said, "Get Gil. Immediately."

Lem said to Murdo, "Mr. Wieldy won't tolerate a junior counselor who goes primitive. I warn you."

Murdo's grin died, for you couldn't pry him away from Camp Chesunquoik now. "A bunch of sissies," he grumbled. "What's wrong with knocking sense into a guy who won't take it any other way?"

"What's wrong when a chess player kicks the board over when he can't get his way legitimately?"

"I don't see the connection," Murdo said.

"Civilization's like a chess game. It's complicated because it's so varied and rich. And it only works when the players agree that force isn't to be called in when somebody gets disgruntled. Now Mr. Wieldy's a civilized person. His aim in establishing this camp is to see if boys can't get along together without busting up the game."

"What're you going to do with fellows like Gil?" Murdo asked.

"Look, friend," Lem said. "The first thing to ask is, What am I going to do about myself? Let Gil ask himself

104

that question, too. See? Then everything straightens out automatically."

Gil arrived with Blis and both were out of breath. Gil looked serious out of his round eyes. Lem's soreness had disappeared, as if he had taken some of his own medicine. He hardly mentioned Dot or Haru. He asked Gil questions about the baseball managers he had met in Florida. He wanted to know how they got the men to work as a team. I almost forgot what we had come to Lem to do, for Gil was so interesting.

Then just at the end, Lem said, "I may sound like a Public Address System, Gil. You know, the apparatus that carries all over the ship so that the captain can talk to each man. But this is what I want to say to everyone in camp: the thing that makes this camp tick is good-will, wanting others to have a good time as well as yourself. I admire ambition, Gil, or I'd have to move out of this State. I don't blame you for wanting to get on the right side of Haru. It's only natural for you to plan rides for your friends. But it isn't fair to Keetsie, or to the rest of us."

"You said, sir, that we must keep Haru in a good mood."

"Yes, but not at the expense of someone else. Keets has given up certain rights in his elephant, so that we all may enjoy her. You, on the other hand, propose to use the elephant as if she were your private property in an environment belonging solely to you. Now, since you have so much influence with Haru, I want you to go and tell him that you've changed your mind. Tell him that you have decided that Keets should ride. Ask Haru himself to invite Keets and Quizzy and Dempsy to ride with him in the howdah into Hoggset. Tell him that if we beat Hoggset, you'd like him to invite you and Stringy and whoever makes the most runs to ride back, if that is all right with you, Keetsie."

Naturally it was. I thought Lem had done wonders to think it out so everyone would feel good. Haru had the importance of asking us to ride. My guests weren't to be disappointed. And Gil could have some fun, too. It all shows what you can do, if you don't raise your voice.

The game was called for two o'clock, so Silas was giving us lunch at eleven. The Committee for Getting Taddie to Meals on Time had made special preparations for this emergency, and the boy was ready, although dazed, at 10.49, with Dot's help. I'd told Taddie that if he was late, he'd probably miss the ride on Dot.

I was up in the tent when I heard Downy's voice outside. "You in there, Keetsie? Here's a gentleman to see you."

"Not Pop again!" I exclaimed before I could think. I knew Pop would have fits at finding me bat boy instead of shortstop.

"No my dear fellow," said a softish voice. "I am not your father. May I come in?" and in he came. There's nothing I hate worse than being called *dear fellow* unless it's *dear little fellow* and they had to quit that when I topped five feet ten.

"Wait, my dear fellow," he said to Downy. "There," and he handed him fifty cents.

"What's this for?" Downy asked. "You don't owe me anything."

"You conducted me here, did you not? I interrupted your pleasure, did I not? I believe in a fair return. Don't

mention it. Delighted." He waved Downy away and then looked at the cots. "Which one may I trust to sustain me, my boy? I'm not as sylphlike as I was at your age."

I pointed out Forman's cot and he let his weight down gingerly as if he'd had accidents before. He was sylphish compared with Silas but still pretty fat. His head was round as a moon and nearly as bald, with little, little eyes, and lots of cheek. He dug a card out of a wallet and handed it to me with a flourish. I guessed he was an actor, but the card read:

Mr. Gus Rummly
Animal Broker.
N.Y. N.Y.

I noticed a scar down one of his cheeks. He saw I noticed and said, "A leopard did that, my boy. I've got a lot of autographs like that. Playful little things, leopards. Had I not been quicker, he would have cleaned my eye right out of the socket. Now, would you do me the favor of counting these bills?"

I knew now he was a queer duck. He handed me a wad of bills, and I counted them, but there was something about him I didn't like. The money came to five hundred bucks, and I told him so and tried to hand them back. But he waved them away. "Keep them, my dear fellow. Keep them. They're yours. Five hundred is right." Then he heaved a sigh and said, "I don't know why I do this. I always lose money on elephants."

I was startled. So that was it. Well, he had another think coming. It was the first time I'd ever held five hundred bucks in my hand, and various things crossed my mind. Pop would be set up to find I'd made all that profit on Dot. Mother'd be relieved. It would serve Gil right, and Haru too, to learn I'd sold Dot right out from under their noses. I could buy a used car and all my worries over feeding Dot after camp closed would be done. Also Murdo and I and Blis could ride around in the car after camp closed and have a whale of a time. But just the same I knew I wasn't going to sell Dot.

"Know anyone who wants to buy an elephant?" Mr. Rummly asked.

I shook my head and wished he'd take his money and go.

"Nor do I," he said. "It's a terrible habit—buying elephants. Don't let it get you the way it gets me. When I hear of an elephant for sale, I travel hundreds of miles and add one more useless object to my collection." He sighed again and I never saw a man look glummer.

"Cheer up," I told him. "I'm not selling Dot. Here's your money."

Mr. Rummly didn't see the money and said, "No, no, you win in spite of my good resolutions. When I read Mrs. Rummly that newspaper account of you buying this vicious elephant from the circus she said, 'Gus, you must go rescue that unfortunate boy. He don't know what he's got into. I don't know where we'll scrape up five hundred dollars, but we have to. Don't return without it.' "

I was waiting to get a word in and said, "Dot's not vicious, and she's not for sale."

He sighed again and said, "Alas, your youthful ignorance is touching. You don't know this beast like I do."

"You've never even seen her," I said.

"There, there you go again! Of course I've seen her. I was at the circus the very day she went on a rampage and they had to give her a dose to calm her down with a squirt-gun. Don't know her!" He leaned forward and patted my knee, and that didn't make me like him any better. "I tell you, my dear boy, don't risk having that monster around another day. She's a rogue, if there ever was one."

"Don't worry about me," I said. "Dot's gentle as a kitten, and I'm keeping her."

"She *looks* gentle, son. Were you ever in an earthquake? Everything looked gentle till *it* broke loose. I know the marks of a rogue. Did you note how little her eyes are?"

I looked at Mr. Rummly, and if little eyes were the sign of a rogue, I was almost touching knees with one.

"May I ask what rate you have to pay for accident insurance?" he asked me.

"I don't have any."

"Oh, how wicked some people are!" he exclaimed. "To think of saddling that dangerous beast on you without protection of your fortune."

"I haven't any fortune either."

"*What?*" the poor man was sure taken aback. "How do you propose to finance this creature's upkeep?" He wrung his hands as if he was having a pain. "Oh, this is scandalous! Do you know what the courts call it, if this elephant breaks loose and destroys these children I see running around? Criminal carelessness. They could send you to jail for life, and probably that villain will see that you go. He is known far and wide for his jealousy."

"You mean Haru?" I said. "Haru's the best elephant keeper I ever saw," I told him. I wasn't going to let on how right he was.

"How many elephant-keepers have you seen?" he asked. He pulled a paper out of his pocket and spread it open. "Now here's a contract you won't believe," he said.

"I don't want to take your time," I said. "Dot *isn't* for sale."

He didn't hear me and began reading the contract. I wished Silas would blow the bugle. The contract offered me $500 down for Dot and a 10% rake-off on all net profits from resale or renting out of Dot. "Now you read it and see for yourself," he said.

"I guess you didn't hear," I told him. "I'm not selling Dot."

He acted surprised. "Wh-why-why this is unheard of!" he gasped and his cheeks shook and the leopard scar looked redder. "Luckily for you, dear fellow, when I set out to do a kindness, nothing can stop me."

I could have told him he was stopped now, but it didn't sound polite. Just then Silas blew that bugle, and believe me, I hopped up and shoved the money into his lap and said, "That's lunch, if you'll excuse me. We have to go to Hoggset for a ball game."

"I thought something must be on your mind. I would like to see the owner of this camp."

"He's got the mumps."

111

"Then the man who runs it. There must be somebody who can convince you of the folly of throwing a fortune away."

That suited me fine, so I took Mr. Rummly to Lem. At that moment Lem had eleven hundred other things on his mind besides animal brokers, and he polished Mr. Rummly off in no time. He'd seen that kind before. He told Mr. Rummly that he was proud of me for not putting money ahead of my word to Camp Chesunquoik about having the benefit of Dot through the season. Lem said that if Mr. Rummly wanted to make a satisfactory offer, instead of trying to steal an elephant for a third of what it was worth from an inexperienced boy, he could submit the offer by mail towards the end of August.

All this time Mr. Rummly's scar was getting redder and redder. He told Lem that in all his experience he had never met so many narrow-minded people in one spot. He said that so far as speech, dress, manners, brain-power, and want of comprehension went, he knew nothing to match us for plain ignorance and stupidity. He also said that it would be a long cold day before he drove six hundred miles through the contaminated country to do an ungrateful moron a favor. He confessed he had learned his lesson at last and asked us if we would grant him the privilege of sending a doctor at his expense, so we could have our heads examined.

Lunch was getting cold and Lem said, "Blis, I think the gentleman would like to be shown to his car."

"Such black ingratitude . . . !"

112

"Perhaps Murdo will like to help."

Mr. Rummly took one look at Murdo—and went. When Blis came back he was grinning. "He's my definition of an optimist," Blis said to me. "He asked me to tell you that he'd see you after the game."

CHAPTER XI

That ride to Hoggset was more fun than a couple of monkeys because I had three of them with me in the howdah. There's something about a howdah that makes you feel in a good humor. Taddie and Quizzy made jokes I'd never heard before, and Haru was so happy at my not selling Dot to Mr. Rummly, that he acted kind of monkeylike, too. He made Hindu faces and told funny stories about the young of baboons and child elephants. Even Dot joined in the fun. She broke off a leafy branch and held it up for a sunshade.

We set out before the others, but they caught up to us as we neared Hoggset. Their noises must have given the wild life of central Maine the notion it wasn't so wild after all. As Quizzy said, you could have heard a bomb drop, but you'd have to be close.

The parade to the ballfield was Blis's idea. Dot went first, then the truck with the team, then the bus with the rest of the fellows and Lem with Silas and the table-squad in his car. When we hove onto the ballfield, Hoggset roared, cheered, yelled, shouted jokes, and laughed. The whole town was out, women as well as men, the kids, and even ball-crazy mamas holding babies because the baby-sitters were there, too.

The Hoggset team was warming up. It seemed to me they'd grown a lot since we were there. They looked mighty big and confident. "Poor things," Murdo said. "They don't know they're just a bunch of trapped rabbits."

"Snag Wickendorf looks particularly like a trapped rabbit," Blis remarked and everybody laughed.

"Snag's face'd make a piece of lead pipe look timid," Gil said.

Lem showed Haru where he wanted Dot parked, at the far end of the stand. Lem told Haru not to leave Dot for any reason whatever. I soon saw why. Sheriff Wickendorf came parading along behind his badge. His mouth kind of watered when he saw Haru, perched up there in the howdah. But there was nothing he could arrest him for at the moment, so he licked his chops and went on to see if he could find any low-grade behavior elsewhere.

The Hoggsets gave up the field and Mr. Pickerel sent the Chesunquoik Braves out to warm up. The temperature on that lot must've been 100°, so it didn't take long. The boys snapped the ball around like pros. Stringy wore his cap cocked like a fellow who had held out for ten

115

thousand dollars more on his salary. Gil looked dangerous too. Anybody that grim and serious could go a long
ways on his face, and Gil had his arm as well.

As I was arranging the bats, the umpire came over
to shake hands with Lem and Mr. Pickerel. He was tall
and strong and every line of his face said *no foolin'* so
plain that Snag himself wouldn't dare contest one of his
decisions. Even when he said "Good afternoon" to Lem
you could tell nothing would make him change it.

He and Stringy and Snag got together and Hoggset
was to bat first. A good thing, too, for it took the tension
off me. I'd never been bat boy in a major game, and of
course I'd forgot and left my spruce gum behind.

Gil Combs walked out to the mound as confident as
six roosters, in a quiet way. I overheard Mr. Pickerel say
to Lem, "That boy's the coolest pitcher I ever coached.
He's so sure of getting what he wants in the end, that he's
never heard of nervousness."

That worked both ways for me. It might give Gil the
game, and also it might give him my elephant. But I let
bygones be bygones. Gil threw a few to Stringy, the ump
signaled for the first Hoggsetter to step to the plate, and
the game was on.

Their first batter hitched up his pants, dusted his hands,
worked out a firm stance, and gripped his bat. But it was
all waste motion. Gil sent the ball down the groove, one,-
two,-three-, and that lead-off guy swung without ever
getting a clear notion of what passed him.

Their second up was the lean and supple kind who

116

are terrific when they connect. But they must have put in a blind man to show their contempt for Gil. He hunted around through the air like he was playing blind man's buff, and not very good at it. When the ball accidentally did hit his bat, it flew up in the air. Stringy ripped his mask off and pulled that foul in as gracefully as a swan reaching for a waterlily.

That was two down and the town of Hoggset began giving tongue. They howled out instructions but the guy was absent-minded, or thinking of something else. He was still standing there when the ump called *"stee-rike"* and held up three fingers.

"Go in and show them," Mr. Pickerel said as our fellows jogged in to the bench. I picked out Stringy's bat first try and shoved it at him. He limbered up and walked out to face Snag, and I saw how serious it was being a hero. After all the talk, this was it. Stringy wasn't just a boy any more, easy-going and all that. He was grown up all of a sudden. I couldn't see his face, but I knew how he looked, tough and long-jawed and practical, with his life all narrowed down to one point—that ball in Snag's hand.

The pitch came and Stringy hit. It was a sweet smack, a clean fast grounder, and if their short stop hadn't been a double-jointed clown able to scoop it up backhanded and flip it to first upside down, Stringy would have made it.

"Good try," Mr. Pickerel said. "And shows he can be hit."

Forman wasn't so sure and fanned. Sprigg popped a fly to third. It was all over fast and Hoggset did the screeching.

But they had to take it back. The next three Hoggsetters laid their bats against the apple a couple of times but made nothing of it. Gil whipped around and caught the first on a steal to second. Sprigg held the throw and tagged him clean, and the ump signaled him to the bench. Boy did that bite Hoggset! What they called the ump would have shriveled up anybody else, but he acted like it was a rain of compliments. Gil caught the next guy— a hot liner. A wonder it didn't tear his arm loose. The final batter died on first and we were up again.

This time I had a hunch we'd do it. Gil was up. He leaned over the plate, lowered his bat a couple of inches beyond the farthest corner, straightened up, and waited. Snag writhed like a crab-salad victim but forgot to put enough on the ball and Gil connected. Biff! It slammed level to the ground between center and left field for a two-bagger! You should have heard us. Even Dot trumpeted, though I guess Haru told her to, for Gil's sake. Any other time I'd have been jealous.

Our short was up next, the guy who took my place because he'd been playing since he was six. Well, he still acted that age. What did he do but give the air a fancy workout with three feeble fans. Mr. Pickerel asked this failure what Snag had. "Oh, nothing at all," he said back, mighty sarcastic. "It comes at you like a comet with a changeable mind." Murdo said that Quizzy would have

118

known what to do with it. Mr. Pickerel asked the right-fielder who was next up to bunt, and he did, and Gil made third.

Murdo was up and I shouted, "Now, you black-haired bum!" He grinned and I knew he was going to do it. Snag gave him the ball and Murdo slugged. The crack told me they'd have to fish that ball out of Hudson Bay, only their left field raced back and turned and speared it out of the breeze first. No pro could have done it prettier. So Gil died on third and that was that.

The third and fourth innings didn't bring any news. I handed out the right bats, mostly, and nobody jumped me when I didn't. I glanced over at Dot occasionally to see if she was enjoying it. But she was dreaming of India, I guess. Haru had got down and was crouched in her shade.

Gil eased the Hoggsetters off the lot at the top of the fifth, and the scoreboard was still a row of goose-eggs, when Murdo came up and connected. It was a two-sacker by rights, but their right field and center crashed head on trying to catch it. Their funny business gave Murdo third. Sprigg was coaching third and told him to hold it. Mr. Pickerel had our next man sacrifice Murdo home, and we pretty near lamed his back pounding him. The scoreboard sang a new tune: Hoggset 0 Visitors 1. Our next batter got caught, but we took the field feeling fine.

I guess it doesn't pay to feel too good until you're back home in bed. Snag leaned hard against Gil's first pitch and made second. Hoggset's next up connected for a hit

119

and Snagg reached third. That was bad but nothing to what came next. The Hoggset batter drove a ball into Gil's hands. Snag daren't run, but Gil dropped the hot ball and the batter tagged first. Gil tried to make up for dropping the ball by catching Snag off base. Gil's throw to Murdo was fast but too low. It bounced against a stone or something, flew wide of Murdo and rolled way out in front of Dot. Haru reached for it, though we screamed for him to let it alone. But Dot beat him to it. She snatched it up in her trunk and flung it back onto the field.

All this happened so fast that everyone was holding their breath until Dot jumped into the game. Then they laughed. Snag naturally hadn't risked a steal when luck was working for him. The crowd was shouting wise-cracks about Dot's fielding. It was lucky Dot had got the ball before Haru, for if he had interfered, it would have given Hoggset one base and evened the score.

Suddenly Mr. Pickerel jumped up and shouted, "No, *no!* You can't do that!" And I saw the Hoggset crowd jumping up and down and laughing and hugging each other. Then I saw why. The umpire was waving Snag in, and the scoreboard boy was hanging up a 1 for Hogg-set.

Boy, did that burn us up! It was bad enough having them hit Gil without ringing in an elephant to help them score. Gil was standing practically against the ump argu-ing with both fists as well as his mouth. It looked as if he was going to slug the ump. Lem and Mr. Pickerel ran out to stop the murder. So Snag and his gang raced after them to back up the ump. So our fellows tore in from the the field to rescue Gil. I loped after them. The noise and name-calling would have done credit to a mob, though nobody had drawn blood yet because they wanted to hear the ump.

He looked as cool as an early frost. He had dragged the rulesbook from his hip and was telling Gil what page and section to read before he went off his nut. The ump held the book about three inches from Gil's face and said, "There it is in black and white. *When the ball is in play and is interfered with, the runner is entitled to one base.* That is the situation here. The ball was in play. The ball was interfered with. The runner, who was safe on first, was entitled to one base. So second moves to third, and the man on third goes in. There is nothing to dispute."

"Yi, yi, yi!" Gil jabbered. "You better go home, and I mean the nut house!" He was the most earnest I'd ever seen him.

"Watch your mouth!" the ump warned. "I can throw you out of this game."

Lem wedged his way to the ump. "I'll take over, Gil."

"He's crazy!" Gil shouted. "Does it say elephants in the rules? No, nor bats or squirrels! If a toad nudges the ball everybody walks in, according to him! Call the ambulance!"

"Gil, control yourself!" Mr. Pickerel said.

Lem faced the ump. "The rules committee didn't anticipate interference by an elephant."

121

"The ball was interfered with, and I have no choice but to administer the penalty. I didn't make the rules." My, that ump was stubborn!

"You heard the ump!" Snag shouted. "Get back and play."

"Let 'em quit!" a Hoggset fan called. "They're yellow."

"You call us that?" Murdo shouted. "Then you're black and blue," and he slugged the guy, though he was laughing.

The fat was in the fire. Gil pushed over to help Murdo, but Snag knocked him aside, and then everybody got into it. Lem and Mr. Pickerel tried to break it up but not a chance! In a minute there was the grandest free-for-all this side of the Portland waterfront on a Saturday night. I hunted for their bat boy to black his eyes, but I saw Taddie knocked over in the mangle, and had to pick him up so he wouldn't be stepped on.

I heard a lot of voices shouting, "Look out! The elephant! Run!"

They scattered like chickens when a dog jumps among them. I dragged Taddie out of the mess and saw Dot heading into the crowd. She was pushing gently, so far as I could tell from the rear view. Haru was on her neck leaning over. I guessed he was talking into her ear. Then I saw something else as she backed around. Snag! Dot had curled her trunk around his chest, under his arms, and was lifting him a few inches above the ground. And

Snag was kicking and clawing and getting tomato-red in the face and shouting what he was going to do.

The crowd stopped scattering and bust out laughing. Snag, the big he-man, talking so tough and looking so helpless, and Dot handling him gently, like a mother lifting a spoiled child out of some mess it's made. I didn't know how Dot picked out Snag. Maybe she remembered the Wickendorf smell. Maybe that was what Haru was telling her. Anyway it did the trick. You can't fight hard when you're having hysterics. Gil was laughing like a madman. Murdo was bent over laughing and the man he had been slugging was, too. Even the umpire almost smiled.

Lem couldn't help laughing, but he and Mr. Pickerel didn't approve and shouted to Haru to make Dot let Snag down. Haru was in no hurry. He was the only cool one in the crowd. He sat up there on Dot with his arms laced together like an idol and talked to Snag in low tones. I couldn't hear his remarks, but they turned Snag into a torch of fury, and Dot had to swing him a bit to cool him off.

That's when Sheriff Wickendorf pushed through the ring of laughers, and he wasn't laughing you can bet. I'd seen the sheriff mad before, but nothing like this. He was practically smoking hot. He stood bravely about two elephant-lengths away from Dot and shook his bony fist at her and announced what he would do if she didn't let Snag down. Dot pretended not to understand, so he

123

shook his fist at Haru and quoted a few pages from the criminal code and announced what he was going to do to Haru and Dot and the Chesunquoik Braves, if Haru didn't force Dot to release Snag.

But Haru was as dumb as Dot and didn't seem to see old Wickendorf and that's when Taddie couldn't stand it and burst out laughing so hard it attracted attention even from Snag. Old Wickendorf was threatening Lem with life imprisonment, and he had Mr. Pickerel headed for the electric chair, and all the time Snag was yelling to him to lay hold of me. "There he is! Get him. Get *him*, papa! There! No, you old bat, there, *there!*"

Finally Sheriff Wickendorf got it and turned and looked at me. He recognized me from before and shouted. "You're the one responsible for this outrage! You brought this wild beast here! You . . ."

"*One moment, please*, Sheriff Wickendorf!" said a sharp voice I knew well. It was Mrs. Augustus Lirrup, with Asa following her, but not so fast. They had arrived late on account of the speedboat acting up, and Mrs. Lirrup was not in the best of tempers. "What is this, a ball game or a brawl?" she demanded.

"It's that elephant, ma'am!" the sheriff said. "Look at it! *Look . . .*"

"I'm not interested in elephants at the moment," Mrs. Lirrup cut in briskly.

"But my son! Look . . ."

"I'm not interested in your son!" Mrs. Lirrup continued. "I came out in this heat to witness a ball game and

I propose to have one. Now stop this nonsense at once. . . ."

I didn't stay till the sheriff got around to me again, besides I was very thirsty. So I threaded my way through the crowd and found the boy selling cokes. "Why in time don't they drive that critter off the field and get on with the game?" he said.

"Have you ever tried to drive an elephant that's been treated unjustly?" I asked him.

He confessed that he hadn't and said, "Well, I'd like to meet the guy who brought it here. He's spoiling my business. I hear he's one of the boys from that camp owns the critter. Do you know him?"

"Sure," I said. "Is that all the cokes you've got?"

The boy looked out over the field and said, "Looks like the row's over. Snag's got free. Wait and I'll fetch you all the cokes you can drink."

"I'll go with you," I told him. I thought I'd buy Taddie one. We ran out back of the grandstand and he sold me a couple and filled up his basket.

"What's he do with it?" the boy asked suddenly.

"Who?" I'd kind of lost track of his thoughts.

"The guy who owns the elephant?"

"Oh, you mean him," I said.

"Who'd you think I meant? What in heck do you do with an elephant?"

"You'll have to ask him," I said, for I didn't want to let on it was myself who'd lost him money.

"If I got close enough to him to ask him I'd likely

125

punch his face. I bet he's cost me a dollar in trade."

We heard shouts and the boy said he guessed the game was starting again and I could help him carry his basket. So I did, and he asked me to give the fellow who owned the elephant a kick in the pants for him, and I didn't say Yes or No, and just as we were going around the stand, who should sail around the corner but Sheriff Wickendorf! He looked so red he'd sizzle if you dropped water on him and he recognized me right off, though I was pretending I'd dropped something behind me.

"So there you are!" he shouted. "So I've got you at last! Set that basket down and come with me!"

"What's he done?" the boy asked.

"You ask what's he done?" the sheriff repeated. "Where've you been and can ask that? He's created a public disturbance, and broke up the ball game we were winning, and threatened my son's life, and he's a public menace, him and his elephant."

"So you're that guy!" the boy said and I didn't like the tone of his voice.

"I arrest you in the name of the lawr!" Sheriff Wickendorf began, and he dragged some handcuffs from his pocket. "Hold 'em out."

"I'm bat boy," I said. "I've got to get back."

"You're coming with me," Wickendorf said. "Hold 'em out! I tell you."

"Want some help?" the boy asked.

I took one look at him and cut and run.

CHAPTER XII

I'd have made it, too, but for that boy and two men who saw me running and old Wickendorf after me. They spread out and grabbed me and the boy caught up and gave me a wallop and Wickendorf arrived. I couldn't fight four of them and the sheriff thanked them and locked those handcuffs on my wrists. I asked the men to please tell somebody on our team what had happened, but Wickendorf asked them to give him that pleasure. The boy was the bitterest of all on account of the dollar I'd lost him.

Well, that was the worst fix yet. From the other side of the stand came a roar of happy shouts and I guessed Hoggset was making another run, but there I was being marched off to jail. I tried stiffening my legs and holding back, but Wickendorf kicked my calves. I threshed around with my arms, but he punched my ribs. I squirmed and tried to jerk free, but his bony fingers met like rivets in my neck. I was as helpless as a beefsteak in the jaws of a starving wolf.

"You'll resist the lawr, will you, you spoiled rat!" Two shakes and a kick.

"You aim to hold back, do you, you buckle-backed

mule!" A squeeze on my neck and a couple of punches.

"Don't think *you're* an elephant, or even a greased pig!" An assist on the rear.

That was no runs, no outs, but plenty of hits for me. Once I stumbled and he shook me. "No, no, you don't! Not this time, you underdone piece of veal. Every time you try that, you'll spend a fortnight more in the jug."

When I added up all the extra time, it looked like I'd miss the first term of school.

We passed the Hoggset Mansion House, but not a soul on the porch. We crossed the street to the forlorn, unpainted box of a jail with iron bars on the windows. The sheriff opened the door and pulled me in. It was dark in the hall after the sun, but I made out a silent thinnish woman with a broom in her hand, Mrs. Wickendorf. I thought she was probably going to beat me with it in the kindly Wickendorf way. But that shows how you're liable to misjudge people.

"Out of my way, Mariar!" the sheriff ordered. "I've got this public nuisance at last."

I stopped struggling so I wouldn't kick her, but she looked too tired to notice it, if I did. It brought back that day when Lem and Blis and I had asked her some simple questions, which she didn't answer, and Lem and Blis had thought her so brilliant.

"Is No. 1 unlocked?" the sheriff shouted at her.

"I wouldn't know, I'm sure."

"Well, don't stand there like a donkey, open it." He held me till she found the key and then he pushed me in. The cell looked like a room to me, except the window had four iron bars running up and down and a bunk instead of a bed.

"There, you rogue, you've disturbed the peace for the last time this year." He turned to his wife. "Where's Elsie?" I guessed that was the name of the nice little girl who had answered questions for her mother.

"I wouldn't know," Mrs. Wickendorf said.

"You never know anything. I told her not to go to the game, didn't I?"

"I wouldn't know that." And this was the woman Lem and Blis considered so intelligent!

"Well, she didn't see much! This vicious character brought his elephant along to break up the game, the minute it looked like we were getting ahead, and she grabbed Snag around the middle and was going to squeeze the life out of him. What do you think of that?"

"I wouldn't . . ." Mrs. Wickendorf began, but the sheriff cut in and said he had enough counts against me to send me up for ten years and the whole town of Hoggset was ready to testify, not to mention Snag, if he ever got his breath back.

Mrs. Wickendorf kept very calm, as if she'd been used to hearing of her son being squeezed to death by elephants for years. All she said, when the sheriff got done ranting, was, "There's a gentleman was in to see you."

"Who?"

"I wouldn't know."

"Don't you ever know anything?" Wickendorf bawled. "What did he want? And don't say you don't know."

"He wanted to see you."

I almost laughed in their face, she sure was getting the sheriff's goat. She didn't know, either, whether he'd call again, or where he was staying, at the Mansion House or not.

"Now I've got to get back to the game and arrest that elephant, and then go to North Hoggset. Tell Elsie to give him some supper." He pointed a thumb at me. "Bread and water, and maybe some cold potatoes, if there was any left over."

"Please tell Mr. Higgity I'm here." I asked as he pushed his wife out of the doorway and started to close the door.

"I know my business and you tend to yours," and the door slammed. I heard the key turn, and his footsteps faded down the hall, and the front door slammed. My cell was on the street side and I saw his hat pass by the window. I looked out, but there wasn't much view—a couple of stores opposite with faded awnings and ash-hoppers, and part of the Mansion House porch, and a dog asleep in a rocking chair. All of a sudden the loneliness hit me. I'd been living in quite a stir, and now I hadn't a soul to talk to. The emptiness filled my whole inside and throat and my neck ached, though that might have been from the sheriff's fingers.

I tried sitting on the chair, but it was hard and I was sore where old Wickendorf had urged me. I tried the bunk, but that was too much like going to bed. I wished I'd read more, like Downy, so I'd know better what to do in jail. I got to thinking of supper, but I wasn't hungry enough to get excited over cold potatoes. Thinking of food made me homesick for Silas. That very minute he was planning supper, even if he was at the game. I knew we were going to have steak, and chocolate meringue pies for dessert, because it was Saturday.

I tried lying on the floor where it was cooler. I could see I was going to run out of entertainment. There was nothing to do but think, but if I thought about camp, I was lonely for the fellows. I daren't think about Pop and Mother and what they'd say when they heard their only son was in jail. I began to bother about my tent. I was a hot junior counselor, lying on a jail floor. Who'd keep after Taddie?

Well, Dempsy would. I was thankful there was a fellow like Dempsy, willing and reliable and not afraid of being useful. I'd been impatient when he got in my hair for being *too* useful, but it wasn't a common fault. That set me to wondering why there weren't more like him. The human race had been running on for quite a while and going to school and learning fire drills and the exports from Peru. Yet how many Dempsys were there? Not three out of four. I doubted if there were three in four hundred, not among the people I knew and probably three in four thousand, outside of Maine, would be more accurate.

That made me feel blue about human nature, and I decided to check up on the fellows I knew for certain, seeing as I had lots of time, and Quizzy popped into my mind. Quizzy was as dependable as a brick, though not as useful as Dempsy on account of being off with the universe so much of the time. And Downy was dependable, in one direction, anyway. You could rely on him to look up anything in a book.

Then Murdo. He'd run off to the circus and he smoked behind Lem's back, but he was reliable in a big way. He didn't go back on his instincts, which was something, and he'd stopped Haru from kidnapping Dot.

Now *she* was reliable.

Blis, too. You could absolutely bet on Blis. And on Stringy. He was as reliable as a rulesbook. So was Lem, he was reliability itself in a flannel shirt, and I guessed Mr. Pickerel was. I knew Mr. Wieldy was, even if he had got the mumps. And Silas. And Asa. I couldn't imagine Asa unreliable. It couldn't be done.

Suddenly I was feeling good again. Why, I was surrounded by good guys. My blueness lightened up every minute. There wasn't one of them who'd rest before they found me and pried me out of this coop. I felt mighty pleased and comfortable, especially as I'd cooled off some on the floor. It was clean and no livestock running around.

Then Gil Combs came to mind. He was reliable, but in the wrong direction. You could rely on him having his own way. That meant he wouldn't rest until he had wound Haru tight around his finger, and Dot—and it struck me all of a sudden that I wouldn't be there to stop him! That was awful. I'd be shut up day and night in this cell, helpless and worried crazy to get out.

Then it came over me that I *couldn't* get out. I jumped up and pulled at the iron bars, but they were as solid as the wall. I ran to the door and tried it, and it didn't give a mite. I wanted to pound it and yell. I felt I couldn't stand it a minute longer—days and weeks, and nights, especially nights. I chased over to the window again. Maybe there was one loose bar, but there wasn't. But I heard voices and

133

saw Lem walking beside Sheriff Wickendorf and making the sheriff puff, too. Lem was sure heading for me fast, and I felt all choked up with relief.

When Lem got near enough I called to him, and he looked up and waved. "Who won?" I asked.

"We did, 3 to 2."

"Swell! Who made the runs?"

"Come, if you're coming!" Wickendorf bawled to Lem.

My, that news brisked me up some, though I knew Snag would be boiling mad and probably blamed those extra runs on me, too. It seemed ages till the key scratched and the door opened. Lem grinned at me as he came in, as if he didn't hold jail against me. I tried not to let on I'd almost been screaming. It was like Blis said, Lem brought out what you had.

"I'll give you five minutes," Wickendorf said to Lem.

Lem held the scorebook out to me. "You can read the details in your spare time. A close game—tied right to the end of the 9th."

That was Lem's way of breaking it to me that he couldn't get me out. "How long do you guess I'll be in?" I asked, as if it had just come to my mind.

"Till Monday, I'm afraid, Keetsie. Mr. Wickendorf insists that there's no way of springing you legally this late on Saturday, and any other method wouldn't pay." I knew what he meant by that.

"Does Blis know?"

Lem shook his head. "Only Mr. Pickerel. We couldn't

imagine why you didn't turn up when the game got going again, and things were popping too fast to start a hunt. Then when the game ended the big job was to pry our boys loose without a scrap. I wouldn't have dared tell them if I had known. They'd have tried to rescue you, and then we'd be in real trouble with the law.

"I gave Gil permission to ride home in the howdah with Stringy, Forman, and Sprigg. I hope that's all right with you."

"Sure, but how did Mr. Pickerel find out?"

"He was buying cokes for the team and he overheard the boy who sold them crowing over helping Wickendorf arrest you. So I sent everyone on and ran into Wickendorf. I told him how absurd and unjust the arrest is, but you can't talk to the man. He labors under such a burden of accumulated grudges that I'd call him pigheaded, if it wasn't an insult to pigs. When I get back to camp, I'll make a brief guarded announcement that will set your friends at ease without mentioning jail. I can't have the boys writing that home."

"How about Pop?"

"I see no use disturbing your parents since they can do nothing, though of course I'll have to inform them on Monday when you will be released."

"That's right." It was a load off my mind.

"Tomorrow, I'll bring you a basket of Silas's food. Is there anything else?"

The sheriff hove into the doorway. "Time's up," he growled.

With him there I didn't tell Lem I could hardly stand to see him go.

"Till tomorrow then." Lem gripped my hand the extra firm way a fellow does when he wants to say a lot he wouldn't say unless he was a girl. "Get a good sleep. You've nothing to worry about."

"That's what you think," Wickendorf said.

"I can trust you not to do anything rash, Keetsie," Lem said, and I promised and then the key was turning in the lock.

I couldn't have stood it without that scorebook. It was like having the team there, to see what they did. Gil had sure pitched a swell game. It drove me crazy missing that last inning when Stringy got the winning run.

I was out there on the lot yelling for him when someone knocked politely on the door, so I knew it couldn't be Wickendorf, and it wasn't. A nice-looking girl with taffy-colored hair and sky-blue eyes came in with a tray covered by a white cloth. She had such a happy look on her face, you'd never guess she was a Wickendorf, but I remembered her. She was their daughter Elsie.

"There!" She set the tray down on the table. "Mama thought you'd be hungry seeing as you must have had dinner early. So she fried up a steak off a buck Snag got. We'd just as soon you didn't let on to papa."

"I won't, don't worry." Venison in July was as illegal as counterfeit dollars. "How come he won't smell it though?" for it was perfuming the air.

"Papa won't be back from North Hoggset till late, and Snag's over to the Mansion House to supper with a gentleman. There!" She lifted the cloth and I saw a meal that even Silas would have been proud of. There was a big thick steak of venison and brown gravy, french fries, a couple of vegetables, three kinds of pie, several kinds of cake, and milk, but she asked me if I'd rather have tea, coffee, pop, or buttermilk. I told her all I wanted was time. I'd clean forgot I was in jail and had plenty of that.

"Snag sore about losing the game?" I asked.

A scared look came into her eyes as she nodded. "I'd rather talk about the game. If you don't mind company, that is."

She needn't have worried about intruding. It was better than being rescued off a desert island to have any human being there, let alone a nice girl. You should've heard her tell about the game, and she hardly twelve years old! She'd probably caught on to baseball from Snag. Like as not he beat her if she didn't know right off the difference between a curve and a floater. She told me every play, down to the signals and everything, and what kind of a pitch. I wished Pop could have heard her. It makes him so mad when Mother can't remember how many strikes is out.

In between, Elsie got me to finish up the three kinds of pie. She wanted to see if I could tell which one she'd cooked. I just made it, though I had to kind of push the last mouthful down, and I couldn't decide which was best, so I said she made them all, which was correct. I told her I never expected to live so high in jail, and did prisoners always gain weight like I was doing?

She explained why she had to attend to things. She said that her father was like a rabbit dog, when he'd caught the rabbit and dragged it to the doorstep he lost interest. She said the prisoners would have languished there till they were stacked up like cordwood for anything the sheriff would do about it. It made him mad as hops even to be reminded there was a prisoner languishing.

So she had come to look after the prisoners. She enjoyed it. She said she could hardly wait till they got hungry or had washing to be done or socks to darn or letters to write, in case they couldn't write. She hoped I'd have more correspondence than I could attend to. She had liked Haru particularly, he was so illiterate and agreeable. But she couldn't keep any flesh on his bones because he ran it all off at night going to visit his elephant.

"You *knew?*" I was astonished.

"Of course. I let him out."

"*You* did!" I was more astonished.

"I felt so sorry for him. He was so fond of his elephant. Only don't ever, ever mention this, please."

It made me feel good to have her trust me and I promised.

"I knew you wouldn't. I can tell who is reliable. I would let you out, too, but you would have to be back before sun-up."

I felt better when I knew I *could* get out. It made jail a lot more enjoyable, especially with Elsie there. I told her

138

I was so used to sleeping at night that I wouldn't bother to go out."

"I don't see how you *know* I'm reliable," I said.

She looked square into me and she had the nicest eyes and I looked square into them. "I know," she said. "You're like Haru, completely dependable."

Well, that set me back some. If she couldn't tell the difference between me and Haru, she didn't have much judgment, even for an eleven-year-old.

"What's so dependable about him?" I asked.

"I don't know. It's something you feel. And he *did* live up to his word. Thirty-four miles a night, there and back, every night. You can't be much more dependable than that. Now would you prefer to be alone or shall we play checkers?"

I could tell from the way she asked that she was the lonely one. Blis says that I'm the most uninstructed fellow about girls he ever saw, but I knew that much about Elsie, anyway. I told her I'd rather talk because there wasn't much time, seeing as I might be forced to leave jail on Monday.

So she took the dishes and got her knitting and I sat on the bunk while she sat on the chair and it was real homey. I wondered why the people in Hoggset County didn't try for jail sentences oftener since the cooking was better than a hotel, not to mention the company. I wanted to ask Elsie for a decision on her mother, because Lem and Blis were so sure she was brilliant and I was sure of the reverse. But you can't ask a girl if her mother's dumb, even to settle a bet, at least not the first time you meet her.

I hit on a way of finding out more about her father. "What would he do to you, Elsie, if you let me out and I didn't come back?"

I could've bit my tongue the minute I said it. She looked up so scared she was six or seven shades paler. "Please, don't think of such a thing. Poor mama has enough to bear now. Papa would blame her for it. He always blames her for what I do wrong. He says she should have brought me up better. I have to be careful so she won't get punished. I don't like to think of what papa would do."

Naturally I switched to Snag, but that was even worse. When baseball went right, Elsie explained, Snag was lovely. He couldn't do enough for her. He even carried in the wood for the kitchen stove if he'd made a home run or pitched a no hit game, though naturally that didn't happen very often. But when the game went sour, like today, Snag was a terror. Even the sheriff didn't dare cross him. "I can't bear to think what Snag'll be like tomorrow," Elsie said.

"If there's anything I can do, let me know," I told her.

"He mustn't even guess you're here," Elsie said. "I'd be frightened to death. For you and mama, I mean."

"Well, I'll not let the cat out of the bag."

She said, finally, that she must get the dishes washed before the sheriff returned and she asked me what I liked for breakfast. I could hardly wait to tell Murdo what he was missing, so he'd be jealous, for a change. I wished it would be morning in five minutes.

CHAPTER XIII

The bunk was the kind of bed you never quite get to sleep in. I must have been dreaming, for it was afternoon again, and our side was at bat. One funny thing was that we had five men on base, and the umpire was giving Stringy a base on balls without letting either of the two men on third come home.

Snag kept telling the ump the bases were kind of crowded and I was trying to find the place in the rules-book where it says you can have any number of men on base you want, for I wanted to prove Snag was wrong. He had changed his tune by now and his voice was louder. "Awl right, awl right, pal ol' pal, she's in the bag."

"Van," said the ump, only he had a different voice now. "You mean van."

"What's the diff? She's in it. Doan say another word. She's yours. Put her there pal, ol' pal."

I wondered what Snag's remarks had to do with baseball. I wondered so hard that I woke up, yet the voices went on talking. Snag's voice droned on, tough as nails, and the other voice said, "I don't know why I do this." I knew I'd heard that before.

"I know, pal ol' pal," Snag said. "It's because you want the elephant."

Boy, did that jolt me. I knew the other voice now. It was Rummly's. "Here's your fifty," he said. "Or shall I keep it till you're sober."

"Shame on you, I'm sober as a tick," Snag said. "You mentioned three hundred, pal ol' pal."

"My dear fellow," Rummly's voice said. "Three hundred when you deliver. Fifty now and two hundred fifty when you hand over the van with the elephant inside."

I was plenty awake now. I slid off the bunk and padded to the window. I couldn't get my head between the bars, but I knew they were standing in front of the jail door.

"It's an old horse van," Rummly was saying. "The floors reinforced to hold four tons of elephant. I painted *Man o' War* on the sides, then whitewashed over the name. They'll think it's a racehorse inside and not an elephant. Got that in your thick head?"

"So tight it won't come out, pal ol' . . ."

"Repeat my instruction," Mr. Rummly said. "Not so loud."

Snag repeated them but I couldn't hear. It drove me wild. At this minute they were plotting how to cop my Dot, and I couldn't hear enough to make sense.

142

Finally they said goodbye. "Gottasleep," Snag said. "Goo'night. See you." I heard the door slam as Snag entered. Mr. Rummly walked under my window. I guess he was pretty sleepy, too, for he walked straight into a telephone pole. I missed his remarks because there was a noise at the door of my cell.

I thought Snag had tumbled against it accidentally, but he rattled the handle and said thickly, "Lemme in, do you hear? *Lemme in!*"

I had no trouble hearing. I crept back from the window. Soon I heard Elsie's voice in the hall. "Snag! What are you doing? Go to bed, please."

"I want to see the prisoner," Snag said.

"What prisoner?" Elsie asked in her innocent voice.

"That's all right. I know what prisoner. Papa told me."

"Sshh! You'll wake him," Elsie said.

"That's right. I'll wake him—with a baseball bat."

I saw I was a goner if he got the key, but I trusted Elsie.

"Lemme in," Snag said. "All I want's to squeeze him like his elephant squeezed me. I can't breathe right yet."

"Sshh! You'll have papa out here," Elsie cautioned.

"Gimme the key, will you?" Snag demanded. He must have caught her by the arm for she gasped and said he'd break it. I couldn't stand it. He was hurting her. I ran to the door and Elsie gave a little scream. Then Snag made a remark as if she'd stamped on his toe and she got away. Snag boasted a couple of things he'd do to me when he did get me, and they made my blood run cold. I heard a sound as if a heavy body had fallen, and presently I

143

heard Elsie dragging something down the hall. I don't know what the jail would have done without that girl.

I knew I'd not get to sleep for thinking of what Snag was going to do to me, unless Elsie let me out, but she couldn't do that, for fear of the awful things the sheriff would do to her mother. It was a kind of complicated situation to try to sleep on. The town clock off beyond the Mansion House struck one. But which one? It could be half past twelve, or one, or half past one, or half past anything else. There was something for Asa to invent! A clock that told you right out what time it was instead of beating around the bush and letting you wait half an hour to find out. And no birds this time. Then I thought why didn't I invent it, instead of depending on Asa? I'd make millions because people'd be glad to stop guessing what time the clock was hinting at, and I'd be famous.

I must have dropped asleep for another dream came up and even crazier than five men on base. It was Haru calling me to wake up. That was a new one. In most dreams they don't usually let on you're asleep. You think you're awake and enjoying common sense, no matter how screwy the things are you're doing. But in this dream Haru was saying, "Wake up, Worthy Master . . . It is Haru, Worthy Master . . . It is Dot . . . Wake up, please."

That was a good one, as dreams go. What would Dot be doing in Hoggset at half past twelve, or whatever it was? Or Haru. Probably nobody in Maine was happier to have me nicely jailed up than Haru, unless it was the

144

sheriff, or Snag, or Gil. But the voice went on and finally I woke up to make it stop, and the first thing I heard was, "Worthy Master, wake up . . . It is Haru."

Well, I was having a night of it. I padded again over to the window and at first I thought they'd walled me up for I couldn't see the lights or anything. Then Haru leaned down from above and the wall turned out to be Dot standing broadside. The howdah had been taken off, and I could see Haru's turban, and he was saying, "Worthy Master, I am here. Will Worthy Master come?"

I hadn't been worthy mastered so much in a week and it made me feel fine. I thanked Haru for his kindness in bringing Dot to call on me. I asked him to request her to put her trunk in between the bars so I could pat her. This he did and she obeyed and it made me homesick to be free and ride her again and go in swimming. But at least Haru had brought her, and that showed a lot more of this good nature that Elsie and Blis and Asa and everybody else talked about than I had ever noticed. It paid for all the nuisance of being in jail.

"Will Worthy Master come?" Haru asked softly.

"How can I? Don't you see these bars?"

Haru made a remark to the elephant. Dot curled her trunk about a bar and gave a little yank before I knew what she was up to. I heard a funny little sound and—there wasn't any bar. It clinked as she set it down on the pavement.

"Does Worthy Master see?" Haru said, and the white

145

of his teeth outshone his turban. "These bars are for the Queen of all Created Elephants as the yarn that women knit. Watch again."

"No, no, Haru," I cried in a whisper. "Stop her! Quickly. Don't let her yank another. They cost money, and besides, I can't come."

He said a word and Dot withdrew her trunk, but his voice had changed again. He naturally could not understand why I refused his generous offer to escape. "The Jewel of Distant Jungles has journeyed a long way to assist Worthy Master," he said rebukingly.

"I know. I thank her. I thank you, too, Haru."

His voice grew colder still. "Show this gratitude by climbing forth. One step across and thou art saved from this king of hyenas."

I knew by his voice that he had come less to rescue me than to get even with the sheriff. If I didn't help him pay Wickendorf back, Haru would be more furious at me than any time yet. He'd be Gil's friend from now on. He'd never forget my senselessness nor understand why I had to stay. Yet how could I put Elsie in such a fix? Suddenly I remembered my promise to Lem not to do anything rash and that decided me for keeps. I told Haru.

"You will not come?" Haru's voice dropped to freezing and sounded threatening. I thought of Snag and *his* threats. It was dreadful to be pulled in two directions like this.

146

"Thank you, Haru," I whispered. "But I can't. Master Lem would have to hand me back or get Camp Chesunquoik into real trouble. And Elsie would be disappointed in me. You would not want me to hurt her, would you, after she let you out so often?"

"You will be sorry," Haru said. He was good and sore now.

"Please, Haru, before you go. Hand me up that bar."

Haru had gone. Dot simply glided away without good-bye.

I lay down, crushed. I had lots of time to think over what a donkey I'd been. Better if I'd gone and kept Haru friendly, even if I had to be brought back. Nor would I get any credit from old Wickendorf for not going. All he'd see was the open space where the bar had been. I bet it cost plenty, and he'd take it out on Mrs. Wickendorf.

I couldn't lie still and just think. I padded to the window once more. If I tore up my shirt and made a rope of it, the way the books tell you, I couldn't be sure of noosing that bar. It lay flat on the walk. I tried the opening and found I could just wriggle through. I saw that the side of the house was shingles and that decided me. They were dried up and would give my bare toes a purchase so I could climb back. I dragged the chair up and wriggled out and dropped down, though it stung my feet some.

Boy, that fresh night air smelt good, and I was *free!* That was the first time I really *knew* what it was like to be free. I was like a middle-aged fish who'd been swimming all his life and suddenly said to himself, Why this is *water!* Ain't it *swell*. I couldn't go back into that cell, still hot and smelling of three kinds of pie, not even for Elsie. I remembered something else, too—Snag and his threats. He was going to break every rib, one at a time, he had promised faithfully, just like Dot had done for him. Then he was going to knock my teeth down my throat, and so forth. Heaven knows what would stop him. I couldn't. Elsie couldn't. And I didn't believe the sheriff could.

I left the bar lying there and started down the street, still free, and there stood Lem in my way! Not the flesh and blood Lem, just the real Lem that I knew—the Lem who had grinned and gripped my hand and made me want to be the kind of guy he could rely on. I stood stock still and then I turned back. After all, I thought, maybe Elsie wouldn't let Snag find the key, or he might sleep late. I'd ordered breakfast for nine, and maybe Lem would come soon after. I thought of all the things I'd ordered for breakfast and I guess they decided me. I couldn't run out on Elsie after putting her to all that trouble.

I almost didn't get back into that cell as it was. Those shingles didn't curl enough to help my toes much, and it was hard to hold the bar and climb. I had to throw it into the cell and it made an awful racket. I guessed I wouldn't make a good second-story man, I didn't have the knack. When I'd squeezed into the room and tried to put the bar back, it wouldn't stay. Dot's wrench had bent it, just a mite, but enough. That was one on me. Here it was graying up with dawn and I'd wasted a lot of sleep and had to leave the bar on the floor after all.

So far as I know I didn't have any more dreams. It was late when I woke for good, the air was hot already, and I was so empty that I could fold over. It had been a pretty active night, of course, and I'd earned my appetite. One thing was bad, that empty space in the window. I was going to be asked some ugly questions, and I had to figure out what to say. One thing certain, I mustn't let on that Dot had jerked that bar out, or old Wickendorf would go crazy and have her arrested for house-breaking. Yet I couldn't just say it fell out on account of an earthquake or something. I decided to tell them I couldn't explain it and it surprised me as much as anyone, which wasn't stretching it so much at that.

Yet that didn't satisfy me, either. I wondered if it'd pay to throw it out into the gutter or give it to somebody who passed as a souvenir. It worried me so that I couldn't keep my mind on that breakfast and finally I decided to have another go at putting it back. I saw a couple of things then that I hadn't noticed in the dark. When Dot had yanked, the bar hadn't broken off smooth. I tried fitting the tiny jagged slivers at the end into their places in the window part, and it worked fine. It held, and it wasn't bent so much that you'd notice unless you looked close at the top. I fixed that. I lowered the window a mite, not half an inch, so the crack didn't show. Now whoever came into my cell wouldn't know it wasn't as tight as the other three bars, unless they leaned against it and sighed, the way they do in poems.

I fixed it just in time to scramble back into the bunk as Elsie knocked and asked if she could come in. I grunted, and said 'Ga mornin' like I was still three quarters asleep.

"Oh, I'm so sorry to wake you," Elsie said. I yawned and said I liked it and she asked me how I'd slept and I said, "All right, except for a few dreams." I decided not to mention overhearing Snag and Mr. Rummly and her dragging Snag down the hall.

Elsie told me to go wash up while she put breakfast on the table. When I got back I could scarcely see for the steam rising from the porridge and hotcakes and bacon and fried eggs and coffee and the other things.

"Is the whole family going to eat in here?" I asked.

Elsie laughed one of those happy laughs, like a wren on a sunny morning. "Aren't you funny! No, that's all for you, just what you told me you liked. I've more coffee on the stove."

"You had breakfast yet?" I asked, and when she shook her head I said, "That's dandy. Sit right down and we'll have it together."

She hesitated some the way a girl does when she's made up her mind to do something. She was just pulling up to the table when the door gave a sharp squeak. We both jumped, and there was Snag Wickendorf looking in. His face was a wreck, kind of blear-eyed and saggy. His clothes were a mess of creases, for he slept in them. The ugly way he stared at me made me wish I could make a try through the door, but that would be deserting Elsie.

"Where've you hid the aspirin?" he growled at his sister.

"I'll get it," Elsie said. "Soon as I pour his coffee."

"I'll pour it and you get it," Snag said, and the way the words kind of grated out of his mouth I knew something bad was going to happen.

"Now, Snag," Elsie said. "Just because you don't feel good . . ."

"*Get it!*" Snag ordered.

Elsie looked small and helpless beside the big bruiser. Snag was glaring at me. "You remind me of something," he said and held a hand to his aching brow.

"Snag, there's hot coffee in the kitchen," Elsie said.

He didn't hear her. "It's coming back to me," he said. "You . . . Oh! I know! It was your elephant!" He stepped into the room.

"Snag!" Elsie said decidedly. "Now let him alone. He's done nothing to you."

"Oh, no!" Snag sneered. "His elephant only squeezed me so my insides are all misplaced. That's nothing. Nothing at all. I'll see how he likes it, though, and he started towards me.

"Snag!" Elsie screamed. "Stop, or I'll call papa."

"You get the aspirin!" Snag shouted at her. "You'd better bring the mop, too."

I guess I'd never been really scared before. There was only the table between us and he was so slow and sure, even the way he raised his fist.

151

Elsie cried, "Snag, don't!" Her voice went shaky as if she was all but crying. "*Don't*, Snag! You mustn't!" She clung to his arm.

Snag shoved her away so hard she fell against the table and it tilted a little and some things fell off with a clatter. "You mind your business." The noise of broken dishes didn't help his head. I was trying to keep the table between us and dodge through the door when he came around, but he saw that and slammed the door. He stepped at me and took a slug at my face but his other fist got my shoulder so hard I spun around.

Elsie jumped at him screaming, "Papa! *Papa!*" but he slapped at her and would've got her, but I hit him on the jaw which jarred his headache considerable.

That's when he got dangerous. Elsie managed to pull the door open and cried, "Run! Run!" But Snag beat me to it and he knocked her back into the room and slammed the door shut with his foot. Then he came after me in earnest.

I threw the chair in his way, but he heaved it against the door. I tried to push the table between us, but he knocked me down. I tackled his legs, but he kicked loose. Elsie jumped at him which gave me a chance to get to my feet. But he threw her off and was backing me towards the window to polish me off when I saw the bar and my head came clear and steady.

"Touch me and I'll brain you, Snag!" I shouted and grabbed the bar and pretended to give it a terrific wrench to break it loose. It came easy, naturally, and I sidestepped

Snag and brandished it in his face. The look he gave that bar was something to see. I patted him on the head with it. I guess I was excited and patted him harder than I intended, for down he went on his knees, slowly, like a calf they're counting on for veal. Elsie's mouth opened in a scream, but no sound came out. By then Snag was all relaxed on the floor, out nice and cold.

Elsie stared at the bar and gasped, "You're w-w-w-wonderful!"

"That's nothing!" I said as if I snapped iron bars loose every day.

"But to *think* of it, I mean! Just when you were being killed!" Her eyes were so shiny with tears and admiration that I wished I didn't have to explain.

"It wasn't anything, really," I said. "You see, Elsie . . ."

Sheriff Wickendorf's head appeared as he shoved the door open and I stopped explaining. He looked kind of the worse for wear, too. He stared at Snag lying so peaceful on the floor, and the dishes around him, and Elsie looking at me with awe and clasping her hands in joy. "What in halibut's going on in here?" he asked.

"Oh, papa, papa, it's too wonderful!" Elsie cried.

Just then old Wickendorf caught sight of the weapon in my hand. "What're you doing with that bar?" he asked.

"Papa, papa, listen!" Elsie cried and seized his arm.

A long low groan from Snag relieved me a lot, for it showed he wasn't entirely dead.

"Papa, listen to me, I mean!" Elsie cried. "Snag was going to beat up Mr. Keets. He was so crazy with his headache he didn't know what he was doing. . . ."

"Well, why's he there?"

"Listen, papa. Snag might've killed Mr. Keets, so Mr. Keets had to defend himself, didn't he? It's in the book. Self-defense, I mean. So Mr. Keets grabbed that bar in the window and gave a terrific pull and broke it out and handed Snag a teeny little tap on the head. That's all."

"But it ain't possible," Wickendorf said.

"But he *did!* I saw it. I saw him do it!" Elsie exclaimed.

A longer, louder groan from Snag gave her an idea. "There, papa, asked Snag, if you don't believe me. He ought to know what hit him."

I knew enough to shut up, because it would have been

154

wrong to go back on Elsie's story, and anyway old Wickendorf was looking at me with a kind of respect. "The only trouble is, it ain't possible," he kept muttering.

"Show him what you did!" Elsie begged me. "Tear him out another bar and show him, if he won't believe you."

That was a new turn and scared me simple. "No, no! Those bars cost money. One's enough." Then I said to the sheriff, "I guess I've run up a little bill, sir."

Snag was sitting up by now and blinking and his head hadn't been improved by my little tap, but he was a bit more cautious. "Hold him, hold him, papa."

"Elsie says this boy bust loose that bar and slugged you with it," Wickendorf said to his son.

"Hold him, will you?" Snag said. "Where in the name of help are your handcuffs?"

"I asked you, did he bust that bar loose?"

"How else'd he get it?" Snag snapped.

"But it ain't possible."

"Oh, my head! Don't make it worse," Snag said.

"Just tell me what I asked."

"Where's the bar now?" Snag said. "In his hand. Where was it? Tight in the window. What do you make of that?"

Old Wickendorf reached for the bar, but I wasn't that simple, and only let him look at the ends. "It's wrenched all right," he said. " 'Tain't a clean break, like as if it was defected. But I still don't believe it."

155

Snag raised himself to his feet but leaned against the wall.

"Watch out, papa!" Elsie cried. "Snag's going to grab the bar."

I drew back and the sheriff said, "I'm not going to believe what ain't possible, hanged if I will." He glanced at the three bars left in the window. "Hang the expense! I've got to see this." Then he said to me. "Pull me out another. Just one."

I thought he had me but I said, "The State of Maine mightn't like it if I went around wrecking jails."

"I'll manage that part of it. Just one, and no more."

"It's like Elsie said," I told him. "Once was all right, in self-defense. . . ."

"I tell you to pull another, if you're so all-fired strong."

"Well, I won't. I'm not in the mood."

"I told you!" the sheriff looked at Snag and Elsie. "He won't pull another because he can't."

"Papa, I *saw* him!" Elsie exclaimed. "So did Snag."

"Let the old fool believe what he likes," Snag snapped. "You can't tell him anything."

"No more you can," old Wickendorf said. "Not if it can't happen."

"You can't even get Pop to fasten him up so he can't attack me again." Snag pressed both hands to his head and said, "If it wasn't for my head, I'd be able to think. Pop, come here a minute."

I didn't like the turn things were taking. I wasn't out

of the woods yet. I heard Snag tell his father to snatch the bar.

"No you don't!" I said. "The law isn't going to like it when it hears I was assaulted in my own cell."

"That's right, papa," Elsie said. "You could lose your job."

Suddenly a voice broke in calling, "Anybody home?" It was Lem and I called right off, "Here I am, Lem! Come in!" When that State-of-Mainer's face appeared, with Blis and Asa following, I took the first breath I'd had in fifteen minutes.

It was funny watching their surprise. They had expected to find me lonely and languishing, and what they saw was different. For once Blis looked as if he didn't have the full explanation at his tongue's end. Lem's a great one not to ask questions. He just stared.

"Oh, I'm so glad!" Elsie exclaimed and burst into tears.

"I'm sorry we have so depressing an effect," Lem said.

"She's been under a strain," old Wickendorf said. "She's had to look on while your boy tried to brain my son."

"Indeed!" Lem said and I heard Blis draw in his breath. Elsie stopped a sob and said indignantly, "Papa, *papa!* That's not so!"

"You tell us," Lem said to Elsie.

"I'd just brought in Mr. Keets' breakfast, and Snag came in, and what he promised he'd do to Mr. Keets

157

would have scared any other boy to death. But Mr. Keets kept his nerve and tried to stave off Snag without injuring him, but Snag was too strong for him. If Mr. Keets hadn't grabbed that iron bar and pulled it loose from the window with his own two hands, so as to defend himself, it might have been very serious."

"I see," Lem said quietly and walked to the window. Blis and Asa went, too, and examined the roots of the bar. I knew the time had gone for explaining. I couldn't any more call Elsie on her story than I could blab on Haru and Dot.

"That clears everything up nicely, thank you," Lem said to Elsie. "Sheriff, did you also witness Keets snap the bar in two?"

"No I didn't, and wouldn't believe it if I did."

"No," Snag said sourly. "You can't fool Pop."

"What do you mean by that?" Lem asked.

"What do I mean?" Snag snarled. "The bar was in the window. Even Pop would admit that. Then it hits me on the head. How, you might ask? I didn't do it. Elsie couldn't do it. So the bar jumps out by its own self and slams me out cold, or else *he* did it. And I saw him to do it. So you can't lay it to the bar. That's what I mean."

"Papa wasn't here, so he has no right to say Mr. Keets didn't do it," Elsie put in.

"All I'm saying is that it ain't possible, that's all," old Wickendorf grated out. "But if he did do it, it just backs up what I've said from the first, the boy's a menace, him and his elephant, a public menace. I just wanted to learn

158

him a lesson not to create a public disturbance with his elephants and such. And what's he do! He starts to tear the jail down and cracks my son's skull open, and stands there threatening me with his bar. I'm through with him. I can't learn him and I admit it. So take him away. He's a dangerous character and I don't want him on the premises, so the sooner you take him the better."

"Please, please do," Elsie begged. I sure was unpopular around that jail.

Lem isn't one to miss a trick and he said solemnly, "I'll be glad to comply with your request. But it isn't quite as easy as you imply. There is one small matter you haven't mentioned, though your daughter hints at it. Keets must have been seriously endangered by your son before he would exert himself to the extent of snatching that bar in self-defense. Rather than have Miss Wickendorf appear in court to testify against her brother, I think we both had better drop all charges. Perhaps you and I can draw up the necessary papers, and Snag can witness them. Meanwhile, I gather that Keets has not had his breakfast. We have brought food, and I suggest that Keets eat while we are winding up this unfortunate affair."

Well, they agreed. Blis and Asa lugged an enormous basket of food into the kitchen and Elsie and I had our breakfast together after all. Just before we finished, she closed the door and her voice dropped to a whisper. "Promise me one thing," she said, very sweet and quavery, and I said I would, what was it? And she said,

"Promise me you will never, never breathe one word about Dot breaking out that bar, and I won't, either."

I was plain dumfounded. "*You* knew that?" I gasped. I'd almost come to believe I *had* done it and was feeling pretty good about it, and now she had to spoil it all.

"Of course I knew it," Elsie said softly. "I heard Mr. Haru calling and calling and I thought you'd never wake up. I heard the bar drop on the walk, too. And I heard you refuse to escape. It was n-n-noble of you."

"You heard all that!" I was glad she had, in a way.

"Certainly, but nobody else did. So now Snag thinks you broke that bar out, and papa doesn't know what to think, and it's best to let it go at that. If they think you're that strong, they may leave you alone."

"You sure are a good li . . . I mean story-teller!" I said.

"I told only the truth!" Elsie said. "I never said you snapped the bar. I kept saying you pulled it, and you did."

"But you were so surprised, yourself, there at first."

"Of course. I was surprised you thought of grabbing it and fooling them. Now please promise you won't ever tell."

"I promise. But Haru knows and he'll chirp."

"Now Mr. Haru isn't going to let on he was helping you break out of jail," Elsie said. "He's far too sensible for that. I do hate to have you go. But Snag's very forgetful and might take a crack at you tomorrow. So I would try to avoid him in the future if I were you."

Lem knocked and looked in and said it was time to

160

leave. He had said goodbye for me, he added, and I saw he'd picked up the scorebook. We walked at a good pace to Asa's boat in case Snag might change his mind, seeing as I had to leave the bar.

CHAPTER XIV

Nobody said much until we cast off and headed down the lake. Then Blis began, "We've been patient, Keetsie. Let's have the low down on that jail bar and your new-found strength."

"You heard Elsie," I told him. I wasn't going back on my promise to her if they threw me out of the boat.

"I heard her. So what?" Blis retorted. "Any idiot knows you didn't snap an iron bar with your hands."

"You heard Snag," I said.

"All right, I heard Snag. Out of kindness I will not comment on his intellect, even before you warped it with that bar."

"If you won't believe two eye-witnesses, you won't believe me. Besides I promised not to tell."

"I approve of that," Lem said.

But Blis is romantic and he had to dope out how it happened to suit himself. He decided that Elsie fell so hard for me that she smuggled in a saw, at the risk of her father's displeasure, and I spent the night sawing my way out. Then, because I had fallen so hard for her, I hadn't the heart to escape after all.

We got a good laugh out of that and then Asa said, "That's a pretty and touching story, only it smells of cheese and has more holes in it than most cheeses. Where would an eleven-year-old girl locate a metal saw at a moment's notice, presuming she could recognize one? What would she and you do to drown the noise it made? How would you explain your unusual actions to passersby? What saw ever left splinters sticking up? How could you bribe Snag to make that earnest confession of seeing the bar yanked out? And why would a candid little girl like Elsie resort to perjury? That explanation's as thin as the beef in a roastbeef sandwich."

"You explain it then," Blis said.

"I haven't the necessary data," Asa said calmly. "Possibly the bar was defective in some way we could not see. Possibly it had been broken before and that outfit was too lazy or slovenly to fix it. I find myself agreeing with the sheriff, that it was impossible, but happened, which is simply the unscientific way of saying we haven't the facts."

I wanted to stop this so I said, "It's my turn to ask the questions. How did you ever get the game going again, when everyone was so mad?"

"That's another unscientific statement," Lem said. "Nobody on the Hoggset side was mad, except Snag, because they got a run, thanks to Dot, and rather enjoyed seeing us mad. Then we made a bargain with Snag that he would call off his father and get the game going if we induced Dot to set him down. Which is what happened. By the way, I saw Rummly in the crowd. Did he ever say anything more to you?"

That jolted me, for I'd forgotten Rummly. "He did, though he didn't know it," I said.

"That makes your usual sense," Blis said. "How could he talk to you and not know it?"

So I told them about being wakened up and overhearing his offer to Snag if he'd deliver my elephant to him in a horse van.

Blis laughed hard, for him. "You say they'd been quenching their thirst at that hotel?"

"Yes, considerably."

"Wonderful!" Blis said. "If Dot is never threatened by anything worse than a horse van, she'll lead a long and happy life."

"I agree," Lem said. "I doubt if we'll ever hear from Rummly again."

"Then that leaves only Haru to worry about," Blis said.

"Who's worrying about him?" Lem grinned that grin of his which dissolves everything that bothers you.

Asa smiled, too, and said, "Which side's Haru on now? I've lost count."

"Let's see," Blis said thoughtfully. "Dot was Haru's pal from infancy. Then Keets buys in. Then Haru kidnaps her back. That puts him anti-Keets. Then you make Haru's voice and swing him back to Keets. Then Gil threatens no Florida and Haru's back in the Combs' camp. Then Lem takes a hand and Haru turns pro-Keets for the ride into Hoggset. So he ought to be still pro-Keets unless Gil has made a new bid in our absence."

I wished I could tell them how swell Haru had been to bring Dot to rescue me from jail. But I couldn't, so I didn't explain why Haru was now twice as mad as before, and back in the Combs' camp, as Blis called it, for keeps.

All this time I was enjoying the ride and the freedom. I'd not seen Lake Chesunquoik down the middle length-wise before, and it was beautiful. The woods sloped up from the lake to the mountains beyond. According to Asa it was wilderness and bulged with bears, deer, skunks, and so forth. We came in sight of camp too soon for me. Somebody saw us and everybody collected and it was quite a reception.

"Well, we got him," Lem said, "and you'll hear all about it. I notice that you like to write short letters home. You can make this Sunday's letter still shorter by omitting any reference to the fact that one of our popular junior counselors spent Saturday night in the lock-up. It might give your parents wrong impressions."

They laughed and Forman said, "Are you censoring the letters?"

"No, my friend," Lem said. "This is the Camp with a Difference. We do not believe in censorship. We do not practice blind coercion, either. We prefer each of you to see things in the right light. Let me turn on a little more light. We now have a waiting-list at this camp, and I don't mean only the boys who are waiting for Taddie . . ."

They howled at that, and I looked around for Taddie but didn't see him. He was probably still dressing for breakfast.

Lem raised his voice, "I mean that there are thirty-six boys eager to replace anyone who resigns from Camp Chesunquoik, or leaves for any other reason. So if I have a letter from anyone's parents referring, however casually, to this incident, I shall promptly return their son by way of reply. He can spend the rest of his summer at home explaining how Keets was arrested by Sheriff Wickendorf on the charge of disturbing the peace with his elephant. That elderly official could not see that Dot actually *kept* the peace by suspending the game—and his son—until all had quieted down. However Keets was well looked out for in jail by the sheriff's delightful daughter . . ."

Loud raucous noises rose, but Lem held out his hand. "Miss Wickendorf will be twelve next year and your remarks are irrelevant. Dinner will be in twenty minutes. After dinner I wish to see the junior counselors in the bungalow. We soon start our wilderness trips."

They let out glad yells and we went ashore. Lem invited Asa to stay to dinner. I shook Stringy's hand and congratulated him on the game. It sure was good getting back to my tent and being a junior counselor again.

Sprigg called me "jailbird" but Dempsy was the only one who took it seriously. Forman wanted to know how many cockroaches I'd had in my cell. I told him none, and I had rarely seen better housekeeping anywhere. He asked a few more questions and said, "Jails must be running down. Not a rat. Not even moldy bread. Nobody bothering to bake files in cakes so you can saw your way out. No rope made of your shirt and the sheets. You must've been bored to death."

I had no complaints on that score, I told him. It was a pity I couldn't let on what happened, and he'd have felt better about jails.

Only one thing made me sad. Haru did not speak to me when we went to dinner. Gil was very nice when I congratulated him on his pitching.

Murdo told Lem that Mrs. Lirrup had invited Mr. Pickerel to pick out the camp's worst boy and bring him over to dinner.

"And he didn't take you?" Lem asked.

Murdo grinned. "He took Taddie. He thought he'd play a trick on her."

I don't believe I ever saw anybody laugh more hearty than Lem. "Trust Pickerel!" he said. "He's got a sense of humor worthy of this state. I'd like to hear what goes on when Mrs. Lirrup sees that cherub-face. If she can turn up anything bad in him, Harvard ought to give her a degree. Taddie's not a walking timepiece, but I don't find another fault."

"He likes his own way," Murdo said.

167

"So did George Washington," Lem shot back. "Show me someone who doesn't and I'll give you eleven million dollars as soon as I earn it."

The dinner bugle interrupted before Murdo got Lem's offer in writing. Silas outdid himself on that feast. Sprigg said there were fewer legs of lamb running around Chesunquoik County especially with brown crisp fat on them. Downy said it would be worth being a lamb if you could associate with Silas's gravy. It gave Haru a dreamy look after one mouthful. Silas had also invented a new dessert in honor of my return from jail. It was a meringue the size of a cantaloupe with five kinds of filling and layers of ice cream between each kind. Nobody I heard raised a single objection.

Before we dispersed Lem read the results of tent inspection. The ratings were based on the tent's neatness and cleanliness and so forth. Spaceship got top score with 85, First Base next with 80, and Ant Heap fifth place with 60. Everybody clapped, while they laughed, when Blis's tent's win was announced, and Blis tried not to look pleased, because it is kind of sissy to be as neat as 85, even with Quizzy to help.

But nobody laughed when Lem said that the best-scoring tent would have the privilege of Dot's company and assistance, and Dot's owner could accompany her on any trip he so desired, which naturally made me feel good. Ordinarily, trips would start on Tuesdays and return on Thursdays, and there would be baseball and hobbies on the other days. Lem said that he had yet to hear of another camp this side of the Ganges run on such luxurious lines that elephants were provided to carry the duffle, haul the firewood, and wring out wet shirts if needed.

"Camp Chesunquoik is truly the Camp with a Difference," he said. "Its owner is so retiring that he is never seen. Its cook fattens boys while you watch. Its work squads have to be fed sedatives to keep from overworking. Its baseball team has won every game it has ever played and has an elephant for mascot. And its most junior junior counselor has been thrust into jail for keeping the peace. I mention these excellences modestly," he added, "because these triumphs are largely due to you, rather than the management, and Mr. Wieldy is grateful to you for them."

You could trust Lem Higgity to make you feel good when you deserved it, and vice versa. The fellows went to their tents for Rest Hour and we junior counselors sat around the oval table in the bungalow for discussion. Mr. Pickerel had thought of everything before going over to Mrs. Lirrup's. He had mimeographed lists of what to pack for our trips, maps, instructions as to what to do in emergencies and in between. But this meeting was principally to discuss a trial trip for Dot.

Asa had been asked to attend, and now I saw why. He had suggested that we spend this experimental night at a forsaken lumbercamp beside Lake Lilypad on the Lirrup property.

"Mrs. Lirrup will like that, or not!" I said to Blis.

"Don't be a dope! She's inviting us."

"Two weeks ago we were worse than poison to her."

"You'll never understand women," Blis said. "So don't try."

"What is there to understand? I know they're supposed to be changeable, but this doesn't make sense."

"Your mind has the elasticity of a block of concrete," Blis said. "Now that Mrs. Lirrup has determined to expose boys, she wishes to be thorough. She realizes, and rightly, that she can get an enormous amount of original material from the spectacle of you, for instance, trying to camp out in the wilds with five ill-assorted tentmates, a Hindu, and a sensitive elephant. Particularly if it rains."

"Does she think she's coming to?" I snorted.

"No, Mrs. Lirrup is leaving tomorrow for Boston for a librarians' convention. But Asa has put his recorder on wheels, and no doubt it will take notes for her. Whatever plans Mrs. Lirrup makes will be adequate, as you ought to know. Now listen to Lem."

Gil was sitting on the other side of me and leaning forward with his arms on the table so he could listen better. I noticed a little book in his hip pocket and pulled it out to see what he was reading. He was so intent on Lem that he never knew. The book was only about Maine's hunting and trapping laws. I wondered why Gil bothered about them. Then it opened to the flyleaf and I saw something that made me go cold. There was Snag Wickendorf's name and Gus Rummly's address in pencil underneath.

170

I nudged Blis and held the book under the table, but so he could see. "How do you suppose Gil rings in on them?" I whispered.

"Put it back," Blis said.

"Why . . . ?"

"Put it back, and don't dare mention this," Blis insisted.

So I did, and Gil was listening so seriously, he didn't notice.

Lem was reading the names of the counselors to go on the trial trip with Mr. Pickerel. "Blister . . . Murdo . . . Keets . . . Haru . . . and Asa Lirrup, if he so desires. That party is large enough for this experimental journey."

Gil cleared his throat, the way you do before making an impressive speech, and said, "Has Haru spoken to you yet, sir?"

"What about? He's always speaking to me," Lem said.

Gil cleared his throat again. "Owing to my future plans, it will be necessary for me to go on this trip."

"Necessary?" Lem repeated. "Why?"

"Because I must learn all I can about elephants before taking Dot to Florida."

"This is news," Lem said. "Keets, have you sold Dot to Gil?"

"No."

"Have you any intention of doing so?"

"No, and I never will, and I've told Gil so a dozen times."

"Thanks," Lem said to me. "That should clear the situation up. Gil, you hear that Keets will not sell Dot. Therefore you will not be taking her to Florida. Therefore it is not vitally necessary for you to acquire any more elephant technique than the rest of us. Therefore the need of your accompanying this party is not pressing. Therefore the list will stand as read. Is that finally clear to you?"

Gil flushed up, but he said patiently, "Let me explain a little more fully. Mase, my father, has a wonderful collection of wild animals. He does not buy them. He accepts them. That is one of his rules. They must be given to him. I like to give him something special on his birthday, which is on August first. I have never been able to afford an elephant. But now that I have an opportunity to get an elephant reasonably, it will be a glorious surprise to him and . . ."

"Just a minute," Lem said. "Did you hear Keets say that Dot is not for sale?"

"Yes, sir," Gil said. "Nearly everyone who wishes to sell us an animal begins that way. They think they can get a higher price. There was the occasion when Mother wanted to give father some twin kangaroos . . ."

"Let's stick to elephants," Lem said.

"I merely wanted to state that she got the kangaroos, sir," Gil said. "I anticipate no difficulty in purchasing Dot."

Lem was beaten. I'd never seen a State of Mainer beaten by a Florida boy, and it was sad. Lem hadn't another word to say except to dismiss us, but I heard him muttering to himself.

Gil, however, said, "Then it will be all right for me to go on this trial trip?" he asked, as if he had convinced Lem.

"No," Lem said, and he sure held himself in remarkably. "Not this time, Gil." I was sorry for Lem, for he spoke so gently I was afraid his spirit was almost broken, or he would have destroyed Gil then and there, the way he almost destroyed Mr. Rummly.

But he didn't even dampen Gil's spirits. All Gil said was, "Well, I'll be ready," as if Lem had already changed his mind.

I didn't trust myself to speak to Gil, so I went with Blis to the dock to see Asa off. Blis was laughing quietly about Lem being so flabbergasted by Gil's persistence. But Asa said, "There's a certain grandeur about it."

For the first time since I had known Asa's speedboat she wouldn't start. Asa peered here and there, the way you do, and couldn't find what was the matter. "She's been acting up lately," he said. "It's awkward, for I must run Mother in to Hoggset tomorrow for the train."

"Lem could take her," Blis said.

"Not on that road." Asa continued to inspect the works.

"It's usually wet ignition in the end," Blis said.

Asa stared across at Little Yellowstone and considered the wind. "My tools are over there. I guess I'll paddle her over. It won't be the first time."

173

"We can tow her with canoes," Blis offered.

"Don't be silly," I said. "Use my elephant power. Dot can tow her over in no time, and we can help Asa find out what's wrong."

Asa agreed and, even more important, so did Lem. I think he liked my using Dot for something Gil hadn't thought of. Haru was asleep, for he observed the Rest Hour you can bet. Lem wasn't quite happy about our taking Dot without Haru. On the other hand he wanted to show Haru that he was not indispensable.

Luckily it was Rest Hour, because we were kind of new at hitching elephants to speedboats, but Dot understood, and the trip was simple. I rode Dot. I sat facing the rear and holding the tiller while Blis and Asa paddled to show Dot the way. The boat pulled easily, with the wind helping, and we had a successful crossing.

Before we reached the shore we heard a man's voice calling, "Taddie! . . . Ho, Tad-die . . . Where are you?"

Mrs. Lirrup met us, notebook in hand. She did not seem surprised at our arrival under elephant-power. I don't think anything would have surprised Mrs. Lirrup except the discovery of a good boy, and that was the last thing she wanted—nothing to expose, no copy.

"That *imp!*" she cried happily the moment Dot got her footing and started to land. "What a time! I've got *pages!*"

Mr. Pickerel's voice sounded fainter. "Tad-die . . . Taddie . . . answer me . . . Where are you?"

174

"Is Taddie lost?" Blis asked.

"Mr. Pickerel fears so," Mrs. Lirrup said jauntily. "But of course he isn't. Mr. Pickerel hasn't studied the darker phases of boy character very thoroughly, I am afraid. He seems easily taken in." It was then that Mrs. Lirrup really noticed Dot, looming beside her and streaming from every wrinkle, and said, "Dear, what does this mean?"

CHAPTER XV

By the time Asa had made the speedboat fast and explained Dot's presence, Mr. Pickerel's voice had faded
away. Blis was much concerned. It was almost time for
the geyser to erupt, and Young Faithful's blowing off
steam announced feeding time to the bears. It was no
time to have Taddie roaming the woods, or even Mr.
Pickerel, for Evangeline was still jealously guarding her
cub.

Asa was as worried as Blis and he had the speedboat
on his mind, too. But Mrs. Lirrup held to her idea that
Taddie knew what he was about. "He's pure mischief!"
she cried delightedly. "I know him like a book. He thinks
he has found a new way to tease us, and I, for one, decline
to be taken in."

"Mother, it's the bears," Asa said.

"I know bears. I hope they scare him thoroughly. Tad-

176

die's simply hiding out somewhere until we're driven to desperation, and then of course he will return."

"Taddie's a child, Mother," Asa said. "Even men can get lost back there."

"See if I'm not right, dear," Mrs. Lirrup said. "He'll come, but I hardly expect him until he's got the whole camp looking for him. I suggest that they disappoint him and don't start a search. I tried to dissuade Mr. Pickerel. I keep forgetting how nervous men are."

"You've looked on the observation platform?" Asa asked.

"Naturally, dear. Mr. Pickerel took him up there before lunch and promised him a sight of the bears at feeding time. But that way would have caused us no trouble, as Taddie knew."

I hoped this hard-heartedness would change Blis's opinion of Mrs. Lirrup, whom he admired so much, but he called it self-control when other women would have had hysterics, and admired her all the more. But that didn't keep him from doing something. He insisted that Lem should be notified at once and decided to paddle back to camp. Asa volunteered to go after Mr. Pickerel before he got hopelessly lost. I said I'd stay with Dot. Asa forbade me to stray off into the woods. That suited me because I'd been almost eaten by Evangeline that other time. Mrs. Lirrup said she had preparations to make for her trip and instructed us not to feel alarmed about Taddie. "I simply refuse to humor the child in that fashion," she said and went indoors.

177

Dot had drained off and was steaming comfortably in the sun. It was quiet with everyone gone. Suddenly Young Faithful's roaring off startled me so that I nearly jumped into the lake. I could never get used to living by a geyser, but it didn't worry Dot. She had studied Indian philosophy, I guess.

After the geyser calmed off and Dot was taking a nap there in the sun, swaying gently and making her usual noises, like freight cars coupling, I decided I could leave her for a minute. I wanted to see the platform Asa had built in the big tree near the Lirrup garbage heap where the bears came for bread. I told Dot to stand still until I returned and stole back to the tree.

The air still smelled sort of Flittish, and everything was as quiet as a cemetery, except for a funny little scraping noise. I couldn't place it. It sounded like a chicken scratching on sandpaper but it came from above, and the Lirrups didn't keep chickens. The leaves of the tree hid the observation platform until you got under it. Asa had built it cleverly. He had covered the exposed surfaces with bark. I was secretly hoping I'd find Taddie up there after all, even if Mr. Pickerel had looked, but he wasn't. Then all at once I heard a laugh right out of nowhere. It would have scared Silas because it was the way a ghost would have laughed, only pleasanter.

"That you, Taddie?" I called, though I felt spooky calling to nothing.

"Sshh! You'll scare him!" It was Taddie's voice and it sounded from up the tree, but I still couldn't see him.

178

"Where are you?" I called.

"Here, up on the platform."

I edged around the tree and saw both of them at once, Taddie and the bear cub. Taddie was lying flat down on the platform, leaning over, and reaching down to pat the cub's head. It was the cub's claws that made the scraping sound.

"Don't do that!" I said sharply.

"He's coming to see me."

"Don't touch him. He can take off a finger as easy as a buzz-saw."

The cub was curious and not a bit afraid. It humped itself up the trunk the way a boy would.

"Climb down before he scratches you," I said.

"I don't want to come down."

"The mother bear will think you're threatening her cub."

"She'll be wrong," Taddie said and didn't budge.

I didn't know what to do. Evangeline was sure to turn up soon.

"Look, Taddie. Can you climb out on that long level branch behind you without falling off?"

"I never fall off."

"Start now and show me."

"No, I want to see him," and he swung his hand close to the cub's ears.

A low rumbling sound made me look behind me and I jumped as if the bear was reaching for me. It was Evangeline. She wasn't that near. She was leaving the woods

179

on the far side of the garbage pile, but I'd seen before how fast she could move and was scared.

"Taddie! She's come!" I said in a half-whisper. "Don't stir. Hide low the way you hid from Mr. Pickerel, and I'll hurry to get Mrs. Lirrup. Mind now."

For once Taddie thought well of my advice and scrunched together on the platform, and I headed for the cabin. I rushed into the kitchen calling for Mrs. Lirrup. She was upstairs and said she couldn't see me now.

"It's Taddie! He's up on the tree platform!"

"I knew he was being naughty according to his nature."

"But the cub's with him and Evangeline's sure to attack him."

Mrs. Lirrup came to the head of the stairs. "How provoking that you boys never give my bears a minute's peace!"

"Have you a gun?" I called.

"What an infamous accusation!" Mrs. Lirrup cried. "Does your mother keep a gun to shoot her friends with?" Mrs. Lirrup ran down the stairs. "Now where did I leave that notebook?"

"Please, Mrs. Lirrup. Taddie may be torn to pieces."

"Nonsense! Evangeline has a better use for her time. I *wonder* where that notebook can be." She started upstairs again.

I started to run back to Taddie and then thought of Dot and I hurried to her. She was dozing comfortably

180

and I wished Haru was there. I had never felt more friendly to Haru than in that jam. He could make Dot save Taddie. I remembered the time she'd played the game of hyenas and squirted water to drive us away. She might drive Evangeline off too, but how was I to make her understand?

I woke her and led her into the water and told her what I wanted, but nothing happened. I was half crazy with anxiety about Taddie. "Look," I said to Dot and I leaned over and filled my mouth with water and squirted it out in a good squirt. "That's it. Do that." But she didn't catch on.

I daren't waste any more time, so I told her to lift me up, which she did, and I directed her towards the tree. A lot had gone on since I left. Poor Taddie must have thought I'd deserted him. Evangeline was swarming up the tree trunk as if she was going to a fire. The cub was scared to death because Evangeline was grunting out what she was going to do to it, and he was scrambling over the edge of the platform but not getting purchase enough with his short hind legs to give him the final push. And Taddie! Good boy Taddie was already half way along the level bough and working out farther every minute, slowly and carefully, the way Taddie would. Pretty soon the bough began to bend down.

"Hold tight! Take it easy!" I shouted. "We'll meet you at the end."

Suddenly Dot wheeled so fast that I almost slid off and

she galloped away. I was afraid she'd been panicked by the bears. "Whoa! Stop! *Dot!*" I shouted and it made no more difference to her than a buzz of a fly.

That was the awfullest moment! I couldn't desert Taddie, yet I couldn't stop her. The awful part was that it showed me I could never do without Haru. She might have headed into the woods, and then where would I have been? "Stop! *Stop!*" I shouted but she was already in the water. I knew I'd have to roll off and swim back, no matter what happened to my elephant.

She stopped just as abruptly and thrust her trunk down deep into the water and sucked up a good part of the lake. Then she wheeled and back we galloped to the bear tree at a good clip. All this was so fast and exciting that I couldn't guess what next. Dot ran around to the side of the tree that Evangeline was swarming up, and just in time. The cub had mounted the platform and was now following Taddie, as fast as a scared bear could, and Evangeline was kind of doing the crawl stroke trying to claw up onto the platform and tearing off great swatches of it in her hurry.

Well, Dot braced herself and let go! A hook and ladder company couldn't have done better. Evangeline stopped clawing and hugged tight to the tree to keep from being carried away in the flood. Even the spray that fell back nearly smothered me and Evangeline looked like a drowned cat, only bigger. I expected Dot would tear back to the lake to reload, but she knew better. Tad-

die was way out on the limb by now and the cub's extra
weight was bearing it down, so he had to hug tight to
keep from sliding off the end.

Dot pushed her way through the branches right under
Taddie, and I reached up and got a good grip on him and
told him to let go. He did, little by little, and I set him

down on Dot's neck. She backed out of the leaves into
the sunshine and looked real pleased at herself. Taddie
didn't even seem scared. "I saw the bears, anyway," he
said.

Mrs. Lirrup was coming from the cabin. But she
stopped every few steps to set down something in the

notebook. Almost at the same moment, Asa emerged from the woods with Mr. Pickerel. The relief on his face as he saw Taddie, was good to see.

After we'd told what happened I said to Mrs. Lirrup, "Now you've got something good to put down about boys. Taddie kept his nerve through it all."

"*Nerve!*" She held the notebook and wrote it down. "The very word I wanted. Nerve! I should say he had. He interrupts our chess game, upsets the Sabbath quiet, distracts my son, and disturbs the bears at their meals. What of Evangeline's digestion?"

"Look, look!" Taddie cried. "She's punishing him."

Evangeline had indeed called the cub back to her and was boxing its ears.

"*They* know how to bring up children, I'm glad to say," Mrs. Lirrup remarked. "I cannot say that we benefit by their example." She turned to Mr. Pickerel who was mopping his brow. "Let us resume our game. It was my move and I was about to take your queen."

I guess Mr. Pickerel had had enough for one day, for he said we must be getting back. I didn't like leaving Asa alone to find out what was wrong with the speedboat, but he wanted it that way. Blis said later that nothing happier could befall a born engineer like Asa than to have something go wrong with the machinery. There was only one thing better, and that was for him not to be able to find out what was wrong. Blis said that the biggest thing we could do for Asa was to pray he'd have to be up all night to get it fixed in time to take Mrs. Lirrup to the train. He

184

asked me if I'd ever seen Asa look more contented, and I had to admit that I hadn't. Blis said that if we were really Asa's friends we'd hide parts of the engine so that Asa would be forced to invent other and better ones. I told him I thought that was carrying friendship pretty far, but Blis said I knew little about inventors.

"There's one thing I can't make out about Haru," Blis went on. "He seems suddenly more hostile to you than ever, for no reason at all."

I wished I could tell Blis about Haru trying to help me out of jail but you can't keep a secret by not keeping it, so I said, "I never realized until I couldn't make Dot do what I wanted over there that I have to have Haru. I'm really going to try to make friends with him for keeps."

"I like to hear you say that," Blis said. "But we've got to win him back to the idea you can be friends first. He's forgotten his voice, but maybe he can remember his face if he sees it often enough."

"What're you talking about now?" I asked.

"I could draw his portrait and make it a little flattering."

"Swell!" I said. "That would keep him away from Gil while you're drawing him, too."

"I can do him in one pose after another. He'll be fascinated. I can even put Dot in some of them. Don't let on that you know anything about this," Blis cautioned. "It's high time that Gil was coming to earth. If we can kind of scoop Haru out from under him, it might dent his confidence. I'm glad that Lem recognizes that the situation is critical."

"Is it worse than usual, do you think?"

"It's like Maine in election years," Blis said. "As Haru goes, so goes the elephant. I'm afraid that if Gil gets too obstreperous to stay, Haru might follow and Camp Chesunquoik would be out a mascot."

"But they can't take Dot," I said. "It's as Lem says, I still own Dot, and nobody can make me sell her, and Gil's no thief."

"Haven't you learned yet, that there's a way around *everything?*" Blis asked.

"Show me a way around *that.*"

"I can't, and that's what makes me uneasy. For there *is* a way, you can be sure, and Gil is the boy to find it. So one thing is certain: we must secure Haru permanently. This now-we-have-him and now-we-don't is too unsettling and it can't go on for long."

Mr. Pickerel paddled alongside and said, "Taddie has agreed not to mention this bear business at camp, and I prefer that you don't. Or else the boys will be sneaking over there to see if they can't get into danger."

We promised, and landed. Lem was down at the dock to welcome us and Dot, for he had been uneasy about letting the elephant go without Haru. Haru and Gil also appeared and Haru was black as a coalbin. He glowered at me and said something to Dot that made her very downcast. She didn't take time to drain off but followed Haru.

186

Gil came over to us and he was pretty exhilarated. "You made a serious mistake not taking Haru with you," he said to Blis. "He was angry to find that you had taken advantage of his nap to snatch Dot."

"I'm the one to rebuke," Lem said, with some sarcasm.

"Haru is furious at not being consulted," Gil said.

"Haru is not dictating camp policy," Lem told Gil.

"He's so upset that he refuses to go on the trial trip with Dot unless you allow me to go."

Lem's chin began to stick out. "Then we shall have to do without him."

"I advise you not to anger him further." Gil started away.

"One minute, Combs!" Lem said, without raising his voice, but his chin stuck out like a bird roost. "I don't think you realize how deeply committed Mr. Wieldy is to having a harmonious atmosphere at this camp. If you persist in causing discord, he will almost certainly ask you to leave."

"Then Haru would leave, too—with Dot."

I thought Lem would sound off but he didn't. "We have been over this until I should think it would have penetrated," he said to Gil. "Dot stays till purchased. Can you take that in?"

"Certainly."

"She is not for sale. Do you understand that?"

"Certainly," Gil repeated drily.

"There's a prison term for anyone who steals her. Is that clear?"

"Of course."

"Then stop making these ridiculous threats. We are grateful to you for bringing the boys here. We value your pitching. We like your brand of junior counseling. And we appreciate your eagerness to give an elephant to your father on his birthday. But you've got to stop badgering Keets about his elephant, and you've also got to stop influencing Haru adversely. Now I advise you to go to your tent and think all this over, for I'm not bluffing. Nobody is invaluable, absolutely nobody. And nobody is above the laws of cause and effect. If you make trouble here, that trouble is going to turn on you and hurt you. There's nothing so sure. Now will you consider this as a friendly warning?"

"Yes," Gil said and stalked away. He sure was the most confident boy I ever saw, and just about the angriest, in a calm way.

Lem turned to us and said, "I hope he believes what I say."

"Gil's got a single-track mind," Blis said. "But it's a fine piece of track. When he once shifts over onto the main line, he'll go places."

"He'd better make it soon," Lem said. "I know you'll help."

"I've got a suggestion you won't think much of, Lem," Blis said quietly, "but it might do the trick."

"Well, I hope I've not got a road-block in my mind." Lem grinned. "Shoot."

"It's that we take Gil on the trial trip."

188

Boy, that jolted me, just when I thought we'd got rid of him, and I think it jolted Lem. He looked keenly at Blis and said, "You're a funny one. Why wouldn't it confirm Gil in his conceit? Why wouldn't he think that his threats had worked?"

"I don't think there's an ounce of conceit in Gil," Blis said. "Unless confidence is conceit. And those statements you call threats, aren't threats, as he sees it, but warnings of what will come about. Another thing, Gil knows something that we don't know. That's what makes him confident—and dangerous. Therefore it would pay to take him with us if only to keep an eye on him."

Lem thought that over and said, "The point is, what's best for the boy? I don't mind eating humble pie if it will help. But what if he suspects weakness? He'd only be more outrageous than ever."

"Keetsie is going to make an honest effort to keep Haru more friendly by being more friendly to him," Blis said. Then he told Lem about the plan to draw Haru's portrait, and Lem smiled. "So, instead of alienating Haru from Gil, as we've been doing, we might try bringing them both over. And we could make a good beginning by taking Gil with us on the trial trip."

Lem considered. "You may have something, Blis. This will be a trial trip for more than Dot. All right. I agree."

CHAPTER XVI

Blis wanted to go over to Little Yellowstone next day to see how Asa was getting on with the speedboat and whether he needed transportation for his mother. Mr. Rummly was still bothering the back of my mind, although nothing had come of his midnight talk with Snag. I asked Blis if Asa couldn't stop at the Mansion House and see if Mr. Rummly was still in Hoggset. Blis suggested that we both go. That gave me the shivers, because if I ran into Snag I was a goner. Then when we tried to get permission, Lem reminded Blis of some work on the Chesunquoik Buzz he had to do, and I was afraid to say I was afraid to go without him. So it was fixed that I was to go, if Asa would take me.

Blis ferried me over to Asa's in a canoe and we found him working feverishly to finish the boat. A half hour would do it, he calculated, and he had just that.

"*Asa!*" came a voice from an upstairs window in the logcabin.

"Yes, Mother! The boys will carry down your things."

"A-SA, I need you."

"Do you mind going?" Asa said to us. "Tell her that if we don't leave by four, we needn't go, and I can just make it."

So Blis and I went in and called up the stairs. Mrs. Lirrup was less stately and composed than usual. It seems she had turned on the bath-tub and had got so entranced reading her exposés of boys in the notebooks that the tub had overflowed. She had also lost track of the time and was only partially dressed.

We agreed to mop up for her, and she disappeared. Then we heard a shriek, "My suitcase! My suitcase! It's not packed. Stop everything please and finish packing it for me, will you? There's a list on the bureau. I'll dress in Asa's room."

Blis and I dropped mop and towels and rushed into Mrs. Lirrup's room. Chairs, bed, and sofa were spread with plenty of things to go into the suitcase. Blis found the list and said, "I'll read the items and you set the stuff beside the suitcase. Then we can pack it scientifically. The first is—mules."

"Mules!" I said. "I don't see any mules and how'd you get a mule into that?"

"Don't be dense," Blis said. "They're slippers or sandals or something like that."

"Better find out."

191

Blis stepped into the hall. "Just what mules are you taking, Mrs. Lirrup?" he called.

"The pink ones. In the closet."

I darted to the closet, found them, and Blis read the next item, "Old rose stole."

"Stole? *Stole?* What the heck's a stole?"

"Stole," Blis muttered. "What would it be?"

"Don't be dense," I told him.

He hurried into the hall. "Stole, Mrs. Lirrup. Just what . . . ?"

I didn't hear what she said but Blis came back and explained. "It's a long loose scarf, also pink, over the chair. Oh, there it is! No, no, not that, idiot. There. *Here!*" He pulled it off the sofa and I stuck it by the mules.

"Here's one for the ducks," Blis said. "Angora bolero. Ye gods! How do women get dressed! Bolero . . ."

"It has something to do with bull-fighting," I said. "But angora is goats."

"Bolero," Blis repeated.

"I thought women were an open book to you," I said, quoting Blis's frequent boasts.

"Where's a dictionary?" Blis said.

"Ask her, we've only got three minutes."

Once more Blis ran out and came back with instructions. "She says how can she get dressed if I interrupt her every minute. It's a short, loose, waist-length, something or other, jacket, and it's on another chair. There, that one."

"Now what?"

192

"Lavender nylon chambray," he read and gazed wildly around. "I'm goosed if I'll ask her another thing."

"Lavender's the key word," I said. "Maybe that's it," and I slung a lavender something onto the pile.

"Garnet dressing gown."

"That's easy, all we need's a color chart," I said.

He flung the garnet thing at me and read, "White gloves."

"Primer stuff, only where's she hide them?"

Blis yanked out one of the top bureau drawers, and I guess it was greased, for it plopped out all the way and upturned on the flooring, scoring a hit on Blis's toe. He jumped around on one foot while the stuff rolled into different corners of the room.

193

"Dig out the white gloves and hurry," I said. "How much more of the list is there?"

He read, "Christmas nightie . . . my other blue dress . . . most important, white box right side top drawer." That was the drawer that came out.

"Listen, we couldn't pack all those things in a box car," I said. "How is she ever going to get them into that suitcase?"

"You consistently underrate women, Keetsie," Blis said. "It's a fault you must get over."

Just then Mrs. Lirrup appeared. Her arms were filled with things she was carrying from the bathroom. I was up to my neck in nighties, dressing gowns, and so forth. Blis was trying to fold the blue dress. "Oh, no, no, not that one! I wouldn't be seen dead in that!" she cried.

"You won't be seen, if we aren't off in two minutes," Blis said.

"Nonsense, Asa always tries to scare me that way."

We packed and the suitcase lid and bottom didn't meet by three inches when we got the stuff wedged in, even with Blis and me on it.

"Oh, I've forgotten my blue cummerbund!" Mrs. Lirrup cried. "Don't close it yet."

"We're not closing it," Blis said bitterly. "You'll have to take something out."

"But I can't! Surely two strong young men can close one suitcase."

We struggled and the sweat rolled and finally even

194

Mrs. Lirrup saw it was impossible and said, "Oh, I know. The notebooks. They're too precious to trust out of my sight anyway."

So we let go and the lid sprang back, and she dug down to the layer of notebooks. I saw a few titles: PREVARI-CATIONS . . . LANGUAGE . . . EXCUSES (general) . . . Blis called out to Asa we were coming, and the engine was idling when he reached the dock. Blis wished Mrs. Lirrup a successful trip and we left. A little breeze sure felt good after that wrestle with boleros and stuff.

"I do hope I haven't locked my ticket in that bag," Mrs. Lirrup said. She hunted through her handbag three or four times without turning up any ticket. I tried not to think what was coming, but it came. Mrs. Lirrup took the wheel while Asa and I got the ticket. We managed to close the suitcase just before we reached Hoggset. Asa said I'd earned my ride, and I earned it again helping him lug that suitcase to the train. We just made it. Mrs. Lirrup shook hands with me and kissed Asa goodbye, but I noticed she didn't tell him to be good, the way Mother tells me.

"Now for the Mansion House," Asa said. "Do you want me to go in and inquire for you?"

"We'll both go," I said. "Would you hint to Mr. Rummly that I know about his deal with Snag?"

Asa shook his head. "Not unless you think it might discourage him, and I gather from Blis that he isn't easily discouraged."

"No, he's like Gil in that. I didn't know people could stick to anything the way they do."

The Mansion House lobby was empty except for a row of rockers with leather seats and some tired palms. The room clerk looked tired too. He wore elastic bands on his sleeves and he pushed the register around for me to sign without opening his mouth.

"I'm not staying," I told him. "I was passing by and wondered if Mr. Rummly's still in town."

"Who'll I say?" the clerk reached for the phone.

"Talk to him later," Asa told me. "We haven't time now."

"Who'll I say called?" the clerk asked.

"Oh, just say—the Ringling Brothers," Asa suggested.

"How do you spell it?" The clerk pulled a pad towards him.

"Mr. Rummly won't care how you spell it. Good day."

I followed Asa out and he said, "Well, Rummly's here. There may be something in that talk you overheard after all."

I looked across at the jail. I wanted to see Elsie and find out what had happened after we left. "They've put the bar back," I said.

"I wonder if they've removed Dot's footprints," Asa said calmly.

"How did you know *that?*" I asked, and then I saw by the way Asa laughed that he'd caught me.

He slapped me on the shoulder and said, "Don't worry, Keets. I won't give you away. As I figured it, only something as powerful as Dot could have snapped that bar and it must have been defective at that. The joke's on Blis. He's always asking us to use our eyes. I won't tell. So that's the reason Haru turned on you? He was sore because you wouldn't escape?"

"You ought to be a detective," I said.

"I merely list the possibilities and check," Asa said. "How'd you like to run her?" We had reached the boat. "I had to work all night."

I sure was glad I'd come for I'd been itching to get my hands on that wheel. Asa slept all the way home, only he docked the boat, naturally. He was going to take suppers with us till Mrs. Lirrup got back.

Lem announced the trial trip with Dot the next day, but a terrific thunderstorm came up around starting time, so we didn't go. Blis drew a portrait instead. The same thing happened the next day and Blis finished another picture of Haru. Then it rained for a whole day without thunderstorms, and Blis went to town on Haru. Then it was Sunday and he drew some more.

"How many of them pictures do you calcalate on making?" Silas asked.

"Why?" Blis smiled.

"Come and see why." So Blis and I followed Silas to the tent he shared with Haru and it did look kind of congested. There were seven or eight portraits at least.

"See what I mean?" Silas exclaimed. "When I wakes up, there he is staring at me, and it's worse by moonlight. I can't hang up my uniform because Haru's hanging from

197

every hook. I can't see to shave because that big one's propped against the mirror. We daren't leave the front flap open because a breeze'd blow down ten or fifteen pictures of him."

"It'll probably dry up tomorrow and I'll stop drawing," Blis said. "Make him keep them on his side of the tent."

"That ain't all, Mr. Blister. It's not healthy for a man to look at himself like that. When I come in, he's always gazing at how sleek and noble you've got him. It gives him notions, and he slacks on the job. He puts in three-four hours a day worshipping hisself, like he was an idol. If they sold incense over to Hoggset I bet I'd have to smell that, too."

Blis smiled. "I'm sorry you're inconvenienced, but you're helping us a lot by putting up with it, Silas."

"I hope so, I hope so, Mr. Blister. If it'd do you folks any good, I'd let him pin 'em on me. But there's just one trouble about changing people, Mr. Blister. If you can change 'em easy, they'll change back easy. What're you going to do when he loses his appetite for hisself?" Silas waved his hands at the portraits.

Blis said he only crossed one bridge at a time.

"It ain't going to put Mr. Gil off *his* track," Silas went on. "He's a terrible fixed kind of person."

"Yes, but Gil has been a different person these last few days," Blis said.

"So I hear," Silas lowered his voice. "But that don't mean he's budged from what he wants, Mr. Blister. When

198

they can't go along natural, they go underground, that kind does. Mr. Gil's mighty nice, and he always treats me like I had royal blood as I have. But you can't change his mind on getting Dot any more than you can get him to say Florida's just mud and muskeeters. In Florida the fruit falls off the trees into your mouth—at least it bounces off your teeth, according to Mr. Gil, and that's where he's taking Dot, and don't you think different. And the quieter he is the less he'd give up the notion. I know that boy."

Well, that didn't make me very happy, for Silas doesn't talk for the sake of making a breeze. And when Blis and I left him we bumped into Murdo and got another dose of the same. He beckoned us out of hearing of anyone and said to me, "Has Mr. Pickerel told you about Gil's trip to Hoggset yet?" He hadn't, and Murdo looked at me. "This'll interest you, Keetsie. Gil asked Mr. Pickerel if he could ride in with him this morning for the grub. Gil said he had to phone home. Mr. Pickerel talked it over with Lem and they decided to let him. Gil wouldn't talk on the grocerystore phone. He said there was a booth in the Mansion House. Well, he was busy a long time, and what do you think? Mr. Pickerel saw Gil coming out of the jail."

"The jail!" I said. "What was he doing in there?"

"That's what Mr. Pickerel wanted to know. Gil said he had found a book of the Maine Game Regulations, with Snag Wickendorf's name in it, and he'd just left it."

"Did he see Elsie?" I asked.

Murdo grinned. "No, jealous. He said he didn't see a soul. He just left the book on a table. But Mr. Pickerel saw Snag coming out a minute or two later."

"This is bad," Blis said suddenly. "I didn't think it of Gil."

"I don't get it," I said.

"For once I don't blame you," Blis said. "It verges on the obscure. His visit to the Mansion House suggests Rummly. But they're rivals. His visit to the jail suggests Snag. But Snag's working for Rummly."

"Unless Gil offers him a better price," Murdo put in.

"He can't do that," Blis said. "Gil hasn't money. Not to match Rummly, anyway. Besides they all want Dot for different purposes. Gil wants her for his father. Rummly wants to sell her again at a profit. As for Snag, I don't know what he wants."

"Revenge," Murdo said.

"Money," I suggested.

"Let's find out," Murdo said.

"How?" I asked.

"From Gil," and Murdo made a gesture of two hands around a throat.

Blis shook his head. "Not that way."

"We needn't hurt him," Murdo said.

"Nope!" Blis said firmly. "It never works. Besides, I like Gil. I think he's stubborn and too set on having his own way. But still I like him and even admire him, and I won't go in for any bullying." Blis started away.

"Where now?" Murdo said.

"I've got to start the next edition of the *Buzz*."

"That reminds me," and Murdo started in the other direction.

It was great having two friends like Blis and Murdo, and I wished Gil would be sensible and go around with us instead of people like Snag and Mr. Rummly. I couldn't imagine what he saw in them. If he wanted to be mysterious, he certainly was going about it the right way.

CHAPTER XVII

Mr. Pickerel organized our departure on the trial trip in state. Mr. Wieldy had one more day in quarantine, so his tent was the reviewing stand. Dot came first with Haru riding, but no howdah. Her dignity was disturbed some by Silas running out with extra packages of food. We were coming back after breakfast the next day but he was afraid we'd starve and kept thinking of additions that would prolong our lives. Finally Mr. Pickerel stopped him by saying any more packages would break Dot's back. Murdo nearly choked, for Dot could carry an extra ton without even sagging. But Silas got the point.

Stringy was right when he said all we needed was a band. The whole camp collected to see us off. Dot stepped into the water as royally as a princess and we followed in canoes: Gil with Mr. Pickerel in one, and Blis, Murdo, and I in the other. Silas played a bugle farewell, and Mr.

Wieldy shouted *bon voyage* as if we were setting out for Europe.

"I hope the old lady makes good," Murdo said. "I like the idea of shinning up Mount Katahdin on elephant back."

"You've got the picture upside down," Blis said. "When we climb Katahdin, you'll be out behind, pushing."

"If you ever think you see me pushing an elephant up Katahdin, you want to hunt up an eye doctor quick."

Asa was waiting for us at Little Yellowstone. He had mounted his recorder and player-backer, Blis called it, on big wheels with a short axle, so that he could take it on any ordinary trail.

"Who's he going to record?" Murdo asked. "Us?"

"The Maine animals," Blis answered. "Squirrels and porcupines and Dot. He thinks that elephant conversation will mystify the zoologists."

Murdo laughed. "When Dot rumbles they'll think another thunderstorm's coming up."

We turned our canoes upside down in case of rain. It didn't look like raining, but Mr. Pickerel said in Maine that was almost a sure sign it would. He liked Maine weather because it never degenerated into something you could foretell. Haru started talking about the rains in India, but nobody believed him. There wouldn't have been any India left.

Asa led the procession along the old lumberroad to Lake Lilypad. Dot liked the green quiet. Her ears pricked forward and her tail she usually swung sidewise stood still. She took in long-drawn draughts of forest smells. The woods were so quiet that we didn't talk much. Gil was good enough to say it almost reminded him of Florida except for the absence of alligators and cottonmouth moccasins. He missed the diamondback rattlesnakes, too.

The gleam in Haru's dark eyes was silent enjoyment. He could imagine he was in the massive jungly thickets again. You could tell from the way he sat Dot that his pride in her and affection for her left small room for other ties. I didn't mind. More than once Dot had nuzzled me with her trunk to show she was fond of me. All I wanted now was not to be worried by this secret Gil had up his sleeve.

Lake Lilypad was only about a mile from Lake Chesunquoik. When we could see its water glinting through the trees, Asa told us not to make a noise to scare the deer.

"You got a few tied up out here?" Murdo asked. Asa pointed. At first I couldn't see anything worth pointing at, then I saw a movement across the lake. It was a doe feeding on the lilypads and a fawn skipping around kind of fidgety. They were the same brown color as flapjacks and made me hungry.

The lake made me want to be a hermit or a squaw-man or whoever it is builds a hut in the wilderness and lives on what he catches. It was as pretty as Asa said, as I might have known, for Asa never exaggerates. A grove of tall birches had grown up white and tall near the old lumber camp. The roof of the lumbermen's bunkhouse had fallen in and was mossy and rotted, but we were going to sleep under the tent, so that didn't matter.

Another small house stood about twenty feet from the ruins. Asa called it a wanigan. It had been their storehouse and was almost as good as new. Asa said the lumber-

men made it extra strong so that the bears couldn't break in and mess things up. The door was open. Asa started to wheel his recorder in there in case there might be dew. I didn't see what happened, but there was a clatter, and Asa cried out "Look!" Blis told me it looked like a big grayish cat without a tail. It was a bob cat. I wished I'd seen it. Asa was excited. The recorder wasn't on to catch any sounds. "It must be a he," Asa said. "A she would be having kittens in there and be fierce as a tiger."

Gil suggested that we save the trouble of putting up the tent, since it was going to be clear, but Mr. Pickerel vetoed that. He said that we had come out to practice camping in all its phases, as well as to let Dot adjust herself to tents and packs. He would not even let us tie our tent to the birch trees.

It was fun being busy after we got started. Murdo chopped tent poles in the woods. Mr. Pickerel cleared the ground the tent was to stand on. Gil and I cut balsam boughs to use as mattresses, and as we cut them in different parts of the woods, I didn't have to hear much about the inferiority of Maine to Florida. Haru reached down the packs tied on Dot to Blis, who arranged the stores, as he called them, near the place we planned to have the cook-fire.

When Haru had got everything off Dot, he rode her out into the lake. She had fun pulling up water-lilies and passing them up to Haru who made a necklace of them for her. She waded farther and farther out until Haru, who was sitting crossed-legged on her back, looked like a water lily himself, only darker.

"Look at my pet!" Gil exclaimed in admiration. "She beats an automobile all hollow. Where's the Cadillac that'll stand in water up to the roof while it cools its engine?"

Nobody bothered to answer except I overheard Murdo

say to Blis, "How silly can you get?" It was a good sign, I thought. For you can't be bad and silly at the same time, not that kind of silliness. Snag wouldn't have stood for it, or Mr. Rummly. So the sillier the better, I decided, and didn't even notice any more when Gil called Dot his pet.

It took most of the afternoon to finish the chores. We had a contented feeling, though, when the tent was finally up, the balsam bed laid, the firewood cut and piled, our blankets sorted and ready to spread, the food unpacked and arranged, and Dot's hay, turnips, and so forth set out. That swim was fun, after we got beyond the lilypads, and Mr. Pickerel let us stay in till the shadows reached to the other shore.

We drew for the job of chief cook and Blis got it. He took it almost as seriously as Gil would have done. Blis said that thoughtless people considered the dog to be man's best friend. If so, where did they rate cooks? On a desert island which would you rather have, a good cook or a flock of dogs? Take now, he said, which would give you the greatest pleasure, to have Silas saying the steak is ready, or a St. Bernard licking your shins? Blis said an awful injustice had been done to cooks. There wasn't even a statue erected to them that he could think of, yet one of the world's greatest benefactors was the guy who had changed the first steer into roast beef.

"Is something burning?" Mr. Pickerel interrupted.

"Let it burn," Murdo said with a wink. "We don't get talk like this every day."

"I should hope not," Gil said.

"Hold out your plates," Blis said, "and see if every word I've said in praise of cooks wasn't an understatement." He ladled out a gray-looking sort of concoction onto our plates.

Murdo held his plate up. "Just what is this?" he asked.

"Lamb stew," Blis explained. "It's so rich you *baa* afterwards."

Murdo tried some and said, "It tastes like lumpy water."

"Do relieve him of it," Mr. Pickerel advised. "I hate to see it wasted."

Murdo gripped his plate. "No, I'll eat it as punishment for being critical." He didn't stop being critical, or absorbing punishment.

We were too exhausted eating to clean up right away, so we lay there in the twilight and talked. Asa explained an invention he was planning for when condensed power was available. It was to be called the homocopter. It sounded very simple, the way he told it. You just put on wings like an overcoat, attached a little apparatus to your feet, and rose straight into the air.

"I'd like a homocopter's view of what's around us now," Gil said.

"Wilderness," Asa told him. "Mountains, forest, ponds, lakes, streams, deer meadows, and all as wild as Adam. A friend of Mother's flew us over it before Mother bought. When I cash in on one of my inventions, I'm going to buy this region. Then Camp Chesunquoik

208

can blaze a trail over to Mount Katahdin so you'll never leave the wilds."

"I still say, give me Florida," Gil remarked.

Nobody had the energy to think up a sufficiently cutting reply, so we just lay still. Haru wandered back from attending Dot and sat down beside Gil. "At home, Worthy Master, this is the cowdust hour."

Murdo barked out a laugh. "Where's my whisk?" he said.

"Or even your cow?" Blis said. But Mr. Pickerel asked Haru what he meant. Haru told of the cowherd boys getting out their flutes at sunset and starting the cattle home to be safe from the tigers and leopards and so forth. As they shuffled along the roads to the villages, they raised trains of dust that hung in the air, and so it was known as the cowdust hour all over India.

We kept Haru telling stories, partly to cut off washing the dishes, but mostly because it was great hearing about the jungle and young elephants and how their mothers brought them up. Haru's voice fitted into the twilight, and the darker the woods got, the more quiet his voice grew until it was like a shadow of itself, and very strange.

The woods had become caves of blackness, and Blis said that the poor underprivileged bears were waking up and wishing they knew the Lirrups and their garbage heap. Asa finally got up to go. Mr. Pickerel offered to wake him in time to get Mrs. Lirrup from Hoggset if he'd stay, but Asa said he had things to attend to. He showed Blis how to adjust the recorder to register the birds at dawn. That made Murdo laugh. "Tell Blis what dawn is," he suggested.

"Dawn is what campers see as they're going to sleep," Gil said. "I've been out in the woods before."

I thought Asa was brave to walk back that spooky mile alone, but he laughed. "Name me one single animal, vegetable, or mineral that's in a homicidal mood, Keetsie," he said.

"Well, Evangeline, for one."

"You'll have to do better than that. Goodnight, everybody. I'll be back here by ten, if Mother's train's on time."

We got sleepier, and no one mentioned the dishes on purpose. Murdo said, when finally Mr. Pickerel brought the subject up, that we might die in the night, and then we'd have done all that work for nothing. Gil said, "Then there's the rain you prophesied."

Mr. Pickerel said that the rain was still problematical while the dishes were an actuality. You could tell he taught school just by that remark. Anyway, we did them, though we were asleep on our feet. Murdo decided he wanted to sleep outside the tent and I offered to sleep with him, and we took our blankets down to a sloping sandy beach by the lake. Haru went to sleep beside Dot.

Murdo said that we should take watches, for he didn't trust Haru, but he needn't have worried about not staying awake. The beach sloped so it was like trying to sleep on a staircase, only not so comfortable, and the sand turned out to be harder than a good brick floor. Pretty soon the mosquitoes found us. They acted the way you do at a wedding where you wander along a table picking out the food you like best. That's how they sauntered up and down us, taking bites for samples. Murdo jumped up after about an hour of slapping and original remarks and said, "You can stay and be a lunch-counter, but they'll drain you dry and you'll rattle like newspaper." I stayed, but it was lonely in spite of my having all his mosquitoes as well as my own, so I went back to the tent.

They'd tied the flaps back at both ends and rolled up the sides to get air, but there wasn't any moving. Gil was lying crosswise over where I should have been, so I lifted his legs over, and shoved Blis some the other way, and lay down. Sleep closed over me like water, and I sank to the bottom. I heard sounds but they came from the top of the ocean I'd drowned in. Then I heard a terrific noise and I kind of half realized water was slapping me in the face and I woke up. Lightning glared like a million flash-lights and I knew I was awake. A stream of water was hosing me in the face and the wind was blowing and thunder bounced off my head, and I saw we were having the thunderstorm Mr. Pickerel predicted.

"Wake Keets and bring him," someone said.

"Where's the tent?" I asked. I didn't see any sign of one.

"It's probably lit in the Gulf Stream by now," Murdo said.

Lightning blinded us and thunder deafened us and the

wind pushed and the rain poured and then Mr. Pickerel's flash shone on the mass of blankets and he said, "Haru says he'll stay with Dot."

"Will Dot stay with Haru?" Blis asked.

"Come, we'll take our blankets into the wanigan," Mr. Pickerel said. We didn't need to be invited twice. We dredged up the blankets and headed into the wanigan and the bobcat was out of luck. Mr. Pickerel's flash was a lifesaver. The blankets were messy, but we spread them on the floor. We had to close the door because the rain poured in. The lightning showed cracks between the logs, but they didn't let the rain blow in and the roof was good. Mr. Pickerel lay next to the wall, then Gil, then I, then Murdo.

"I wish Asa had stayed," Murdo said. "He'd have been softer to lie on than this floor."

"Be careful not to kick his recorder," Mr. Pickerel said.

"Lucky we brought it in," Blis said.

"If Dot decides to join us, we'll be crowded," Murdo said, and everybody laughed, because there wasn't room for a sardine.

"The first thing I do when I get home, I'm going to spend a night all in one bed," Murdo went on and we laughed again because this was adventure and we felt good and funny.

"I wonder why the bobcat picked this shenanigan for a bedroom," Murdo continued.

"It's called a wanigan," Gil said seriously.

"Go to sleep," Blis murmured.

"Just as you say," Murdo remarked.

A terrific clap of thunder showed the storm was camping right over us. "That was Dot sneezing," Murdo said. "When you sneeze through all that trunk you shake the ground."

I must have drifted off for I started up to find light coming through the cracks between the logs. Mr. Pickerel was snoring and Gil, too, only not the same tune. Blis's face was very intelligent in his sleep. Murdo's eyes were closed but he was scratching and that made me feel itchy. I must've rubbed up against poison ivy, yet it wasn't like that, for poison ivy doesn't jump around on you. Then I was pretty sure it was fleas, because I've been with Blinky. Fleas were the bobcat's problem and the reason why he didn't stay to fight for the wanigan. They were having a field day. After having to burrow through a bobcat's hair for a bite, five human beings laid out like a cafeteria without much on, were a piece of luck.

Voices took my mind off the fleas and I wondered who Haru could be talking to. I made out his voice all right, but the other was hard and raspy. "Come along, soot face . . . hurry it."

"Not one step nearer!" Haru said in a way that made me tingle.

I crawled over Murdo to a slit in the logs, only I stumbled on his foot, and Murdo woke up enough to make a remark.

That wakened Mr. Pickerel. "Less violent language, please," he said.

"Then keep this ape from walking on me," Murdo growled.

The view I had showed me the worst. There stood Snag Wickendorf, looking more like a big bruiser than ever, and he was facing Haru, who stood with his back against Dot's foreleg.

Right then Gil started awake, crying, "What's up? What's up?"

"You aren't, that's a cinch," Murdo cracked.

Blis stirred and slapped himself. "Something's biting me."

"Ouch! Let me out of this!" Murdo said. "It got a piece of me."

"Me, too," Mr. Pickerel said. "Open the door, Murdo. You're nearest."

"There goes another piece! And from a place I can't spare!" Murdo cried.

"Shut up, I want to hear what they're saying," I exclaimed.

"Who locked this door?" Murdo demanded and he pushed hard.

"Make way for a man," Blis said. "I'll open it."

"It's all yours," Murdo said. "Haru's wedged logs against it."

"Snag Wickendorf's out there," I told them. "He's threatening Haru."

214

"*What?*" Mr. Pickerel jumped up and looked through a slit.

"Snag? Did you say Snag?" Gil cried. He was tensely excited. Blis and Murdo found places to look through, but Gil was half beside himself. He kept saying things that didn't make sense.

"Shut up, we want to hear!" Murdo said to Gil, for Snag was ordering Haru to come with him and Haru was backed against Dot.

"I've got to get out. I've *got* to!" Gil said, and then he shouted to Snag, "Hey, Snag. I'm here! Here I am, Gil Combs!"

"He knows you're here and made sure you'd stay," Murdo said.

"You're wrong!" Gil said. "He doesn't know, or he'd let me out."

"Maybe if we all pushed, we could force it open," Blis said.

"Haru's not giving in to Snag," Mr. Pickerel reported. "But what's Snag want?"

"Snag! Snag Wickendorf, here I am—Gil Combs!" shouted Gil.

"Come on, everybody push," Murdo shouted, and we shoved at the door. Then we put our shoulders to one log and pushed till we got red in the face, but nothing gave.

Gil kept shouting to Snag, and Blis and I exchanged glances. Finally Snag turned and swore at Gil to close his mouth. Murdo called, "Come, come, Mr. Wickendorf. We're all gentlemen in here." We laughed in spite of being bitten three ways at once.

Mr. Pickerel leaned against the largest crack and called, "Haru . . . *Haruuuu!*"

Haru looked our way and called, "Yes, Worthy Master?"

"Come let us out please, the door's stuck."

"There are seven logs against it, Worthy Master."

"Bring Dot to drag them away," I called.

Snag turned and shouted at us, "If he tries it, he'll get a bullet through his head."

"The guy's got a revolver, sure!" Murdo said.

I felt hands on my shoulders turning me around and I looked into a face white and contorted. "I must know," Gil said. "Did Snag purchase Dot from you?"

That made me mad. I was so sick of it. "Give it a rest!" I said to him angrily. "Nobody's purchasing Dot. Get that into your stupid head."

"Snag said he could!" Gil choked out. "Snag said he could buy Dot from you cheaper than I could."

"He never tried it. He had more sense," I shouted.

"Keetsie would have pushed his face in," Murdo said, and they laughed, all except Gil.

"I gave him fifty dollars," Gil went on. "I told him Mase, my father, would find someone to give more."

"What in blazes are you talking about?" Murdo chimed in.

"I phoned Mase." Gil turned to Mr. Pickerel. "That

216

day you took me to Hoggset, remember? I phoned Mase from the Mansion House. Father said sure he could find a friend who would like to give him Dot. I was to bid up to a thousand dollars for her, for Mase has plenty of wealthy friends. Then I went to the jail and told Snag."

"Why that's what Mr. Rummly did!" I said. "He gave Snag fifty dollars for the same purpose."

"The old double-crosser!" Murdo exclaimed.

"Oh, let me out!" Gil begged. "If Snag drives Dot off, I'll never see her again."

"How do you suppose I'd feel?" I asked.

"Everybody quiet, I'll talk to him," Mr. Pickerel said. But he couldn't get Snag's attention. Snag was growing desperate. He had obviously counted on Haru giving in to him and helping him drive Dot away, maybe to Mr. Rummly's van, while we were safely stalled in the wanigan. It drove Snag wild to be so near to cashing in and failing. He had thousands of dollars almost in his hands, an elephant driver to manage the beast, and a forest to hide in, and couldn't get going.

"Move!" Snag shouted at Haru. "Bring your elephant or I'll get you sometime when she can't help you."

"That's threatening language, Wickendorf," Mr. Pickerel called. "I can have you jailed for using it."

"Don't make me laugh!" Snag shouted.

"You lied to me! You lied!" Gil said. "Give me back my money."

Snag paid no attention.

217

"The man has no manners," Murdo said. "I've a mind to sick my fleas onto him."

"I'll tell Mr. Rummly," Gil shouted. "I'll tell your father!"

That hit Snag. "Shut your face!" he shouted over. "Or I'll try a little target practice." He moved his revolver to show us he had one.

"Watch out, Gil," Murdo said, for he'd joke with the hangman. "Maybe he can't shoot straight and might get one of us instead."

Snag seemed undecided what to do, and Haru called, "Worthy Master, we await your command."

"Tell Dot to chase him!" I shouted.

"He was talking to me, Keets," Gil said, then he called out, "Stay there and do nothing, Haru."

"Snag, come to me!" Mr. Pickerel called.

Snag had made up his mind. "I'm tired of this," he said to Haru. "Speak to that elephant and tell her to come, or I'll put a bullet through your foot. Then you'll come all right. Now tell her," and he lifted his revolver.

"Worthy Master has spoken," Haru said in that calm way he has.

I knew, then, that it was all up. You couldn't go against a gun. Haru was brave to hold out so long. He was saying something to Dot and held up his hands, like a band leader waiting to start the music. Then he dropped them and the music began with a bang, and it wasn't the tune Snag expected to hear. Dot shoved around and Haru darted out of sight behind her so he was hidden from Snag. Dot raised her trunk to trumpet. Boy, was that a blast! Then she lifted one leg and took a majestic step towards Snag and she swished her trunk sidewise and it would have knocked a house out of her road.

By the time Dot had taken her second step forward, Haru looked around Dot's leg and screamed to Snag. "Climb tree. . . . Don't run, or she run. . . . Climb

quick . . . *queeck* . . . or she squeeze you . . . she squeeze you thin like paper. . . ."

Dot trumpeted the second time, even worse, and took one more majestic step towards Snag, and now her trunk reached for him. That was enough. No man is that brave. Snag took one leap towards the nearest birch. It was as big around as he was and tall, but he swarmed up it like a monkey going after cocoanuts in the pictures. It was quite a sight to see Snag's pitching arm, still holding the revolver, meeting his other arm around that tree, like he loved it, and humping up it, with Dot reaching the tree just as he dragged his legs beyond her. She still trumpeted and blew dust after him, and we cheered like it was Dot trying for a touchdown in the last twenty seconds and getting to the one-inch line. Snag was up thirty feet in no time flat. He held on to the first little limb and he didn't look very dictatorish hanging there like something on a clothesline.

"Can she hold him there while you let us out?" Mr. Pickerel called.

Haru patted my Queen of all Created Elephants and told her to remain exactly where she was and started towards us.

Snag wasn't growing more amiable as he clung to that twig. "Call off your elephant," he shouted to Haru, "or I'll shoot her in the eye."

"She tear up tree then. She mash you like a leaf, but flatter. Little gun no good. Only big gun break through bone." Then Haru spoke again to Dot.

"What are you telling her?" Mr. Pickerel asked, for he did not wish the prisoner to be harmed.

"I tell her to keep gentleman up tree. I beg of her to squeeze him very loving if he comes down. I say now we have breakfast, and she is not to move. She say, Yes, she understand."

Well, that was that. Haru walked backwards towards

220

us so that he could watch Snag and Dot. Neither of them stirred. When he bumped into the wanigan he turned around and pulled away the logs wedged against the door. The marvel was that Snag would have barricaded us without wakening us. When we got out we saw how. A great tree trunk was lying not far from the door and had not rotted, and he wedged logs he had found near the old camp between the door and it. Even a small pole or two would have held the door shut.

Mr. Pickerel took some of the fun out of being free by forbidding us to go closer to Snag. It was just possible that he would feel desperate enough to shoot us in the foot, as he had threatened Haru, in the hope that we would have to leave for help. But Mr. Pickerel made it up to us by saying he and Haru would get breakfast while we went for a swim and got rid of our fleas.

This we were happy to do, except that we found the tent floating in the lake and spent most of our time dragging it back and spreading it on bushes. Breakfast would have been delicious after so athletic a night, but Snag's presence, in his particular position, made it doubly enjoyable.

"Nothing's so healthy as fresh air, especially at higher altitudes," Blis said. "Snag will thrive up there."

Murdo was in a high mood. "I might suppose I'd had a night's sleep," he declared. "Maybe we ought to shift around more, nights, and keep a few fleas. I never felt better rested."

Haru was a new young man and beamed on all of us,

except Gil. He saw that Gil had been partly responsible for Snag's presence and ignored Gil. The rest of us, though, tried to treat Gil decently. He had been fooled by Snag. He confessed that he had not inquired closely how Snag was going to make me sell Dot. That was the part that made Murdo mad. Still, Gil had learned a lesson that might cost him fifty bucks, and I still had Dot.

Mr. Pickerel seemed the least set up and kept warning us that we weren't out of the scrape yet. A man with a gun, even if up a tree, was far from harmless.

We heard Snag calling but paid no attention. "It's delightful to have it cooler after the storm," Blis said. "I can't imagine why he should be so impatient."

"He probably feels he ought to be practicing up for the next ball game," Murdo said, and everybody roared.

"Do we hand him breakfast on a pole, or get Dot to reach it to him?" Blis asked.

"In my country we fast long times," Haru said, and everyone laughed.

We took it easy, talking about the night and laughing and feeling wonderful, and suddenly Blis saw Asa coming out of the woods. We got up and warned him to avoid Snag's tree. He came over and heard the story. He told us the train had been on time and his mother was home with a supply of fresh notebooks. He asked if we had started the recorder. We felt embarrassed because nobody had thought of recorders. But Asa is good-natured and said he would like to register a few scenes, if Mr. Pickerel did not object, and Mr. Pickerel said they might come in very helpful at the trial. I'd not thought of a trial.

"Why should it surprise you?" Blis asked. "What else would you have on a trial trip?"

"Have I permission to break his neck?" Murdo asked.

Cries of "Help! Help!" came from Snag's tree, and we started to run, but Mr. Pickerel stopped that.

Asa hurried into the wanigan to get his recorder, and Mr. Pickerel called to Snag, "What's the matter?"

"I'm slipping. I got cramps," Snag whined in a voice of pain. "Take that man-killer away."

I was afraid Dot had got impatient and was removing the tree, but she was standing at its foot, waiting.

"Throw the gun over there—in that patch of sun, and we will," Mr. Pickerel called.

"It's down. I dropped it when the cramps started."

"Don't you trust him," Murdo said quietly.

"Quick, I'm slipping. I can't stand it," Snag cried in an agonized voice.

"If he shoots, you're witnesses," Mr. Pickerel said and he went towards the tree. I knew then he was mighty nervy. "Where?" he called up as he neared the tree.

"How do I know where?" Snag bellowed. "Under that bush, probably. Look, I can't hold this. Take your elephant."

We saw Mr. Pickerel stoop and search and Murdo said, "Snag can crack him in the back. Let's go help."

Just then Mr. Pickerel stood up and showed us the gun. I felt kind of mean to think Snag was a liar, when he was having cramps all the while. We reached the tree and

Murdo asked Mr. Pickerel to let him see the gun. "Later," Mr. Pickerel said, and after he made sure the safety was on he stuck it between his shirt and his belt, like a pirate.

"I done my part, now take her away," Snag groaned.

"Call Dot, Haru," Mr. Pickerel said. "You'd better take her to the far side of the wanigan."

I looked at the wanigan and saw Asa had his recorder set up and ready to catch anything.

"Hurry, hurry," Snag said, and he slipped a foot or two.

Haru spoke to Dot and she didn't budge. Then he spoke again, in Indian, and in elephant language, and every other language they knew, but still she didn't budge.

A groan came from above and Snag slipped another foot. "Take her, or she'll kill me," he shouted, with some extra remarks that Asa would have to cut out of the tape.

"Speak to her more firmly, Haru," Mr. Pickerel demanded.

Haru ran up to Dot and rubbed her trunk and spoke to her again in strange words. He sounded imperative and then he sounded persuasive. I couldn't tell whether he was ordering Dot to go or to stay. He hated the Wickendorfs so much that he probably didn't object to seeing Snag scared a lot worse still.

"I can't hold it much longer," Snag said weakly and slipped maybe five feet. Dot looked up and eyed him, and suddenly I felt sick. I could see she had no intention of losing her chance at Snag. It was true, Haru told me,

224

that an elephant never forgets, and Dot hadn't forgotten how cruelly Sheriff Wickendorf had parted her from Haru all because of a little parsley.

"Haru!" Mr. Pickerel said sternly. "Get that elephant behind the wanigan, or I hold you responsible for what happens."

"I try! I try!" Haru cried. "She say No. She say she won't come."

"Wait! I've got it! The record!" I shouted. "We can put on Haru's voice!" I raced over to Asa, but he had heard me and was already adjusting the record.

"Tell Haru to go over there towards the lumber camp about fifty yards."

I ran back to the group and told Haru to come. But he was as stubborn as Dot. Mr. Pickerel commanded him and I grabbed his hand, and Blis and Murdo helped, for Snag had slipped again and they saw that something awful was sure to happen.

Asa called to Haru, when we'd got him fifty yards away, "Now order Dot to come to you."

"She won't, Worthy Master."

"Do as I say." Asa was the imperious one now. So Haru made a trumpet of his hands and called to Dot, imploring her to come to him. But she barely looked at him and shook her head and then stared up at Snag. Her trunk almost reached him now, and his face was gray with pain.

"You see? It is useless," Haru said.

"Now, one moment, and we'll see," Asa said, and he turned on the voice.

225

It was wonderful, so clear, so persuasive. It took me right back to the cellar when I was hiding in the stump. "O Queen of All Created Elephants, Gem of the Ganges, and Morning of Thy Worthless One's life, thy hare-brained master salutes thee."

Dot looked in surprise in the direction the new voice was coming from. She could not understand what had happened to carry Haru's voice from where he was standing to this other place fifty yards from her in the other direction.

The record went on and I began to feel cold and hot up and down my spine as Haru growled out, "Oh, thou ungrateful insect, come! *Come*, I say, thou lump of lizard meat. Follow me!"

But still Dot didn't stir. She cocked her head aloft and tried for Snag with her trunk. My hopes fell. If she wouldn't obey that uncanny voice, Snag was doomed. His leg was only six inches above Dot's reach.

Haru said to Asa, "It is no use."

"Don't lose heart so easily," Asa called. "Now repeat what the record is saying at the same time as it says it. *Now!*"

Just then the record got to the real thrilly part and sank to a hoarse whisper. Haru at the same time repeated the words like the record. "Monster of sloth! Hast thou grown fast to the ground? Wilt thou not come? Or must I call the hungry one?"

There was a terrific pause, and I saw Murdo and Blis listening in a spell of wonder. And now both Haru

226

and the record were saying, "Here, tiger, tiger, tiger! Lick thy chops. Thy dinner waits for thee. It cools. Come quickly and eat. Come devour this stubborn beasts!"

Suddenly Haru sprang into the air with a screech. "Quick! Quick! my love! The striped one is behind. He gathers his strength to spring. Save me! Save thyself! *Run!*"

That was too much for Dot. Her head had been switching from side to side, first towards Haru, then in the opposite direction towards his voice. She decided that he couldn't be in two places at once, for elephants are plenty smart, and when both of him shouted *Run* she ran. She galloped—towards the recorder. In her anxiety to save Haru she got mixed and picked up his voice and tore with it behind the wanigan.

Haru speeded after her. No hare ever bounded faster. And Murdo, Blis, and I tore after them. We forgot Snag up the tree, forgot everything. Terror of what was going to happen had changed to wonder at Asa's record and now to hysterics at Dot's flustered mistake. She had stopped beyond the wanigan to see why the voice she was carrying had ceased, and Asa was trying to disengage it from her.

Suddenly we heard shouts. "Help! *Murdo! Blis!*"

We tore back around the wanigan and saw a free-for-all going on. Snag had knocked Mr. Pickerel down and was trying to pull the revolver from him. Gil was punching Snag with all his pent-up wrath.

227

"The big slob!" Murdo shouted. "He didn't have cramps at all."

Snag was too much for them. Before we reached them, he had jerked the gun from Mr. Pickerel, slugged Gil to the ground, and was backing away, waving the revolver at us. "Stop where you are!" he shouted. "Anybody moves gets shot!"

Mr. Pickerel warned us not to move, but Murdo did, and Snag fired at the ground in front of him. "One warning's all you get," he shouted.

He walked backward fast now, and we stood there. He had only a few yards to go to reach the woods. Suddenly we heard a shriek. Haru was screaming at Dot to come back. But my elephant had remembered Snag and seen he was escaping and started after him.

"Call her back!" Mr. Pickerel shouted.

"Don't let her get him!" Blis called.

But it was too late. Dot plunged into the bushes where Snag had disappeared. We stood still in horror, listening to the trees cracking. We heard a shot—and then a scream.

We stood and stared at each other and I was so tense I jumped at a footstep—Haru coming to us.

"You let her go!" Blis said reproachfully, and he shrank from Haru as you would from a murderer.

Haru smiled. "I tell her catch him *queeck*, but no hurt."

"You told her to leave the tree," Mr. Pickerel said, "but she didn't obey you."

"I no tell her that," Haru said, still with his smile warm

228

on his face. "I tell her to go but to suit herself. So she stay."

Murdo gave a halloo and cried, "You win! Look!"

Dot was emerging from the woods, and we saw that she held Snag firmly by her trunk, just as at the ball game. His legs kicked, his arms waved when they were not beating at her trunk, but nothing disturbed her placid approach. Snag plucked at her hold but he might as well have tried to unclasp a boa constrictor. He make remarks which he should not have wasted breath on, and we knew that he was not being unduly squeezed.

She stood before us, holding him, and I say she winked. Murdo says she did too.

CHAPTER XVIII

Well, that was a puzzler for Mr. Pickerel—what to do with a double-crosser like Snag! If he could pretend to be having cramps up a tree, there was no reason why he shouldn't claim he was suffering from appendicitis now, and then let go with his gun.

Mr. Pickerel walked closer to Dot and ordered Snag to hand over his revolver. Snag said he dropped it in the bushes, or mighty few people would be left alive in the vicinity of Lake Lilypad.

"Hand it over," Mr. Pickerel commanded. "You dropped it once before—on purpose."

"You sister of a sheep!" Snag shouted. "I tell you it's back there. When this sister of a sheep reached for me, I dropped it." It made him very angry to be distrusted.

"You shot at my elephant!" Gil said.

"I didn't. I fell over a log and she went off. Now get this hind end of a meatball to set me down."

"Raise your hands," Mr. Pickerel said. "And I shall make the request."

"How can I when I'm being choked by this snake on legs?"

"We shall wait until you do," Mr. Pickerel said calmly.

Snag blazed away at us with a new round of remarks, but presently he raised his hands. Haru entreated Dot to set him down. This she did and loosed her hold on him, but not much, while Blis felt his pockets and Murdo under his armpits. They found no revolver.

"Shall we examine his pockets?" Blis asked.

"Let Murdo do this, while you take notes," Mr. Pickerel said. "We shall have to give a strict accounting to the court."

When Snag felt Murdo's hand exploring his hip pocket, he lost his temper. He forgot that he was in an elephant's toils. But Dot did not relish his announcements and squeezed.

"One fifty dollar bill," Murdo sang out to Blis and handed the money to Mr. Pickerel. Then Murdo tried Snag's left hand pants pocket and came up with a handful of bills. He counted them and said, "Fifty-one dollars."

"Fifty of that is mine," Gil said and reached for the money. But Mr. Pickerel said he would have to prove ownership to the law.

Suddenly Snag surprised us by yelling, "Hi, Pop! Hello there, Pop! This way. You're just in time. Come over here and arrest these pickpockets. They're cleaning me."

Haru gave Dot the sign and she squeezed and Snag's

breath was cut short. So was mine. For who should come out of the trail but Gus Rummly, after Sheriff Wickendorf. Mr. Rummly didn't look happy. Dot caught sight of him too, and stiffened up. She knew a lot more than she let on, good old Dot.

"For once I agree with your son," Mr. Pickerel said to the sheriff. "You *are* just in time. I must ask you to arrest your son, Snag Wickendorf, for carrying concealed weapons, for abusive language, for obtaining money on false pretenses, for the attempted theft and kidnapping of one elephant, for threatening the lives of myself and the members of my party, and on other counts too numerous to mention."

Sheriff Wickendorf interrupted. "Not so fast, not so fast. Who put temptation in the young man's way?"

"That's talking, Pop!" Snag said. "I see you brought one sister of a sheep, and here's another." He pointed at Gil. "Throw them both into the cooler, will you, for attempted bribery."

"I knew it! I knew there was something illegal about this," Sheriff Wickendorf cried and dragged a pair of handcuffs from his pocket. "Step forward, you two," he ordered Gil and Mr. Rummly. "I'll have to do you up together."

"Don't be a goose!" Mr. Pickerel told the sheriff. "Handcuff your son."

"I'm attending to my duty," the sheriff said sourly and stepped towards Gil. "How much did this one attempt to bribe you with, my boy?"

232

"Fifty smackers, Pop, and they've swiped it off me."

"May I interrupt this nonsense?" Mr. Rummly asked in a loudish but gentle voice. "There has been a misunderstanding." He turned to me. "Keets, my dear fellow, I owe you an apology. The younger Mr. Wickendorf made representations to me that he had influence with you—within the law, of course—and could very likely obtain this noble animal for me, in return for which favor I would pay him a small consideration."

"He's right about it being small," Snag said.

Mr. Rummly went on, "Late last evening I was informed by a delightful young person, whose identity I shall not reveal unless compelled to do so by the law, that the younger Mr. Wickendorf had made similar representations to the young gentleman from Florida, for a similar consideration. My usually generous feelings were enraged by this—shall we say, duplicity?"

"Coincidence," the sheriff cut in.

"I also learned," Mr. Rummly continued, "that the younger Mr. Wickendorf's sole influence with you, my dear Keets, was violence. I was distressed. I abhor violence. It is against my whole nature, which is ruled by kindness. I hastened to the sheriff. After considerable argument I got him here in the hope of forestalling unpleasant consequences. I see we arrived too late. I little thought I should ever be the cause of a scene so embarrassing as this. But I am forced to it. Sheriff Wickendorf, kindly arrest your son—as gently as possible."

That was when Snag lost his temper for good and really

233

let go. Dot's ears flapped, as if she could not bear to hear such remarks, and Asa stopped the recorder.

When the sheriff could be heard he was saying, "Not so fast, not so fast, Mr. Rummly. You're under arrest for attempted bribery."

Mr. Rummly didn't turn a hair. "Perhaps I should mention that the Honorable Wilbert Todder, of Augusta, this State, is not only your boss but also one of my most trusted friends. I might also remind you that jobs are scarce. Put two and two together, Sheriff Wickendorf. It is just one of my kindly suggestions."

Well, that took the wind out of the sheriff's sails. The handcuffs jingled, he was so moved. He walked over to Snag, resting there in the elephant's trunk, and arrested him in a lackadaisical way, with Dot tightening up on Snag when he got too violent. But Mr. Rummly still wasn't contented. "The handcuffs, please, sheriff," he said, gently. "Kindly add the handcuffs," and old Wickendorf snapped them on, just as if the Honorable Wilbert Todder was watching.

This all happened so fast that even Murdo didn't add any observations. Dot released Snag. Mr. Pickerel suggested that we start back to camp as soon as possible. I wanted to ask Mr. Rummly if the delightful young person who had put him wise about Snag had the name of Elsie, but he seemed to avoid me. He and Gil appeared to have a good deal in common and talked together.

Like good campers, we left everything in its place, including the fleas. Haru and Mr. Pickerel packed the duffle on Dot like experts. Asa removed the tape from the recorder for use at the hearing. Murdo told Asa that he should play it for his mother. "If she really wants a complete exposé, she'd get an earful," he said.

"I don't think much of that," Blis said, and we all agreed it was a good deal too complete.

When our mixed company trailed back to Little Yellowstone, Mrs. Lirrup greeted us in a new dress and high spirits. "You adventurous dears!" she cried happily. "Did you have a perfect night? Asa tells me it rained, but I can't imagine that we were as inhospitable as all that. Oh!" Her voice changed as Sheriff Wickendorf and Snag caught her eye. "What, may I ask, are you doing again on my property?"

Blis explained to her how Dot had caught Snag as he was vanishing into the woods with Mr. Rummly's and Gil's money, and Mrs. Lirrup felt better. "I've always said that elephants are better for these little errands than bloodhounds. Whoever heard of a bloodhound carrying the criminal back to justice in its trunk? I wonder that elephants are not in more general use."

Asa offered to ferry us across the lake in the speedboat, but Mr. Pickerel declined. "After all, we are giving a demonstration of camping, if a somewhat unusual one. But if you'll escort the sheriff's boat to our side of the camp, it would accommodate us greatly."

"I hope I may be permitted to join the happy party," Mrs. Lirrup said. "One moment, and I'll get my notebook."

I've been in triumphal processions before, but nothing to beat this one. Camp spied us coming before our flotilla, with Dot leading, was half way across the lake, and Lem organized a welcome. The boys lined up back of the dock, so as not to get splattered while Dot drained, and they cheered, and Dot trumpeted, and I was mighty glad that Haru had stood up against Snag, or it would have been a very different homecoming.

I noticed a stranger in a palm beach suit standing by Lem on the dock, and wondered who he was. He had a roundish smiling face and was one of the pleasantest-looking men I had ever seen.

"I've got a surprise for you, Gil," Lem said. "Your father."

"Why, Mase!" Gil exclaimed. "You here already!"

Mr. Combs smiled delightedly. "I couldn't resist coming to see our elephant, after your description of her."

"There's been a slight hitch," Gil said to his father. "I haven't completed the purchase yet. That criminal over there in the boat—no, the one in handcuffs—made false representations to me. Mase, this is Keets, Dot's owner, temporarily."

Did that start my blood boiling all over again! But I controlled myself. I knew I wasn't going to sell Dot, if the Combses offered me all the money in Florida and threw in the state. Dot heard her name and stepped over beside me, and I patted her with one hand while I was shaking hands with Mr. Combs with the other.

He beamed at me like Mr. Pickwick in the movie and

said, "I have never longed to meet anyone so much as you, Keets. Gil never stops writing about you. I hear we have much in common."

I wanted to ask him to name something, but he went right on, "I refer of course to our love of elephants. It has been my lifelong dream to own an elephant. But I have not found anyone able and willing to give me one. As Gil has probably told you, my collection of animals consists wholly of gifts."

I felt more cheerful when he said that, for I knew I wasn't going to give him Dot.

"No nobler animal strides around on this earth," Mr. Combs continued enthusiastically. "No creature has roots that go farther back into the past. I disregard the insects, of course. Gil has written me the romantic story of your acquisition of your Dot—a beautiful name—and your parents have told me what confidence they have in your judgment."

"They have?" I gasped, for that was a surprise. "My parents? You mean Pop and Mother? Confidence in my judgment?" I was stumped. He couldn't mean that.

But he did. "Wonderful people," he beamed. "So quick to understand an opportunity! And to seize it."

I began to feel a little queer around my stomach. "Where did you get to know them?"

"That is quite a little story," Mr. Combs said. Then he said to Gil, "After you telephoned, I got in touch with Major Mountjoy. He has offered to give us Dot. Isn't that delightful?"

I couldn't believe my ears. These Combses! Why didn't they take off my clothes, then and there, and say they liked them? Gil was happy at his father's news, but they hadn't reckoned with me. As soon as I could speak I said, "I'm afraid I can't part with my elephant, Mr. Combs."

"Wait, wait, Keets. The best is yet to come." Mr. Combs beamed all over right down to his middle. "The minute I accepted Major Mountjoy's offer I hopped a plane to Portland. Since I had a little time on my hands, I telephoned your good parents. I explained that I had flown north to purchase Dot and would they grant me the honor of calling upon them."

All this time my heart had been sliding down. "Just what did Pop say?" I asked, hoping against everything natural.

"He said he had a great and lasting affection for your elephant, Keets. He couldn't consider parting with her."

My heart bounced up three feet. "He did?" I gasped. "Pop said that?"

"He asked me out to your home, however, since I had time to kill. What a lovely home you have, Keets, and what a charming, understanding mother!"

"Tell me the worst, please," I said.

Mr. Combs smiled. "There is no worst, my boy, except that your father is rather a stubborn bargainer. Your mother says that you take after him in that. After supper, I was forced to point out that your hilltop must be rather cool in winter for an Indian elephant. I presented,

238

also, an estimate of expenses that an elephant occasions, for food and keeper. But your father would not listen to my offer of $1000. He said that every boy should have a pet, and your mother indicated that her affection for Dot was scarcely second to yours."

"Mother?" I just couldn't believe it.

"Of course they are sensible people, or they couldn't have brought you up so intelligently," Mr. Combs went on. "I knew they must be, living in the State of Maine as they do. So I had come armed with an alternative plan, a sort of partnership arrangement."

"A what?" I asked feebly.

"A sharing agreement, whereby Dot belongs to you forever, although I contract to look after her at times when you are otherwise engaged."

"Swell!" Gil chimed in. "Now why didn't I think of that?"

"In other words," Mr. Combs said, "I agree to pay $1500 for winter rights in Dot, though you resign no claim whatever."

"You mean you buy her and I own her?" I said.

"Your quick mind gets the gist of it at once!" Mr. Combs said proudly. "Your father's lawyer is writing out the terms of the transaction this very day."

"But how did Pop know I'd accept?" I asked.

"When I asked that identical question, he pointed out that you were a minor and still subject to your parents' wishes. He also pointed out that when you came of age you could do your own bargaining. I trust that you will get as much pleasure from the arrangement as Gil and I anticipate."

Just then Silas's bugle sounded first call for lunch, and I woke up to what had happened. Pop and Mother had stood up for me and Dot, and that was so swell that it beat everything else. And Dot was going to be mine forever, and I'd have $1500 in the bank, and could visit her in Florida, and maybe Murdo and I could hitch down to see her in Christmas vacation.

At that moment Lem came back from talking to Haru. He took one look at me, kind of leaning back against Dot with a happy grin on my face, and I guess he must be a mind-reader, for he said, "You deserve it, Keetsie. Now let's go tie on the bag."

CAMP CHESUNQUOIK DIRECTORY

(arranged in order of intelligence)

NAME	RESIDENCE	OCCUPATION
Supreme Dictator, Mr. Wieldy.	The Palace.	Owning this Camp with a Difference.
Slightly more Supreme Dictator, Lem Higgity.	Higgity Hall.	Running the place.
Latest Supreme Dictator, Mr. Pickerel.	The Aquarium.	Countermanding Orders.
Dot, Gem of the Ganges, Necklace of Beauty, Terror of Crocodiles, Jewel of the Distant Jungle, etc.	Imperial Stockade.	Putting up with our assorted insignificances.
Haru Panda.	Broadbeam Villas.	Elephant-sitting in extraordinary.
Silas Broadbeam, Esq.	Broadbeam Villas.	Chef de luxe, and ghost exterminator.

241

NAME	RESIDENCE	OCCUPATION
Bill Lister.	Spaceship.	Editor, Chesunquoik Buzz, art director.
Murdo.	Monkey House.	Head bouncer.
Downy.	Mystery.	Encyclopedia (A to Z plus).
Stringy.	First Base.	Captain, Chesunquoik Braves.
Gil Combs.	Elephant.	Animal Annexer.
Quizzy.	Spaceship.	Authority on Universe.
Taddie.	Ant Heap.	Authority on slow motion.
Dempsy.	Ant Heap.	Chief Stand-in-the-Light.
Forman.	Ant Heap.	Bureau of Critics.
Sprigg.	Ant Heap.	(to be divulged)
Asa Lirrup.	Little Yellowstone.	Inventing while you wait.
Mrs. Augustus Lirrup.	Little Yellowstone.	Author of "Boys, an Exposé."
Keets.	Ant Heap.	Mastadonist, author of "Elephant Toast."

(to be continued next week)